CANDYCE PENTEADO
& MICHELLE NEWMAN

FINDING YOUR Z

AN A-Z ROADMAP FOR
REALIZING YOUR IDEAL LIFE

ISBN: 978-1-66786-659-8

FINDING YOUR Z
Table of Contents

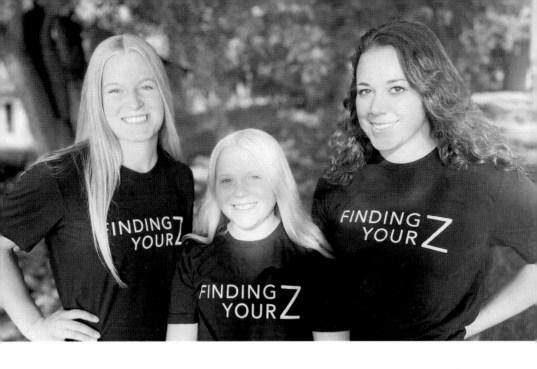

We dedicate this book to our daughters — Liv, Luciana, Bailey, Avery and Finley. Writing this book has been a journey. Thank you for being our biggest cheerleaders and our relentless accountability partners ("*Hey Mom! When is your book going to be done?*"). We hope this book inspires you to go Find Your Z!

INTRODUCTION
Our Journey to Now

Countless times throughout our careers we have encountered people who are "stuck" – professionally, emotionally, personally, and physically – whether they have known it or not. Unfortunately, we have also invested a number of years reading books, administering assessments, and observing workshops that were designed to help these people get unstuck, but they consistently fell short.

Between the two of us, we have over 50 years of experience working in human resources, leadership development, and executive coaching. Trust us when we tell you that most career development solutions fail to help people find real answers to their complex questions. The primary limitations we see are:

1. **They are not holistic.** The most popular career frameworks and workshops being offered to employees only address one aspect of that person's life – their professional life. They don't invite people to think broadly and create intersections between their professional choices and their desire for personal fulfillment.

2. **They are overdone, complex and lack "stickiness."** Meaning people either become overwhelmed or forget what they have learned the minute they leave the classroom, finish the book, or debrief their assessment results. As a result, people don't take action. They feel inspired but they remain frozen and unsure of how to get started.

We knew we had a better solution. We had something that was simple, yet powerful. A framework that can be explained to someone in two minutes and is simply unforgettable: *Enter Finding Your Z.*

THE WORLD TODAY

Now, more than ever, people are searching for purpose and meaning. They want a fulfilling life, not just a life filled with status and stuff. As we are writing this book, we are emerging from a global pandemic that has shaken the foundation of what people previously believed about safety, security, and what really matters in life. People are reassessing how and where they earn income, how they spend their free time, how they care for their loved ones, and where they choose to call home. Things have changed, for all of us. This shift has caused people to ask themselves new questions and consider new possibilities. "The Great Resignation" of 2021–2022 revealed that people were willing to abandon the careers they had spent decades building because they wanted a better life, not just a better job. According to the Bureau of Labor Statistics, the number of American workers quitting their jobs reached an all-time high of 4.5 million people in November of 2021, with no signs of slowing down.

We believe that *Finding Your Z* is uniquely positioned to help people look at their lives holistically in a moment like this. Using the combination of a simple framework, expertly designed coaching questions, and 26 powerful self-reflection exercises, this book will help many people realize their definition of an "ideal life" and get unstuck. In fact, it already has.

HOW THIS BOOK CAME TO BE

This book took us two years to write, but the idea originated back in 2001. Candyce was speaking to a group of summer interns at General Electric and was asked to share her best advice for navigating a career at GE. She decided to give the interns advice for navigating life too and used the concept of an alphabet to symbolize the progression of a career. She suggested that they were somewhere near the beginning of their alphabet right now, and their goal was to get to Z. She encouraged them to consider "Z" as more than their dream job – to imagine it as their ideal life. The presentation struck a chord with people, so she kept using the analogy whenever companies hired her to deliver similar messages.

For over a decade, Candyce shared this concept in classes at GE Crotonville, where she taught thousands of their top leaders each year. One day while on campus, a former student approached her and said, "I can't believe it's you!" He proceeded to explain that he had been in a class she'd taught eight years earlier, along with a person who eventually became his wife. He said that they had been using the *Finding Your Z* framework ever since, and it had helped them create the life they now enjoyed. He wanted to know if she had ever written a book about it. Flattered, she said no, but was so glad it had helped them. A seed was planted that day.

Fast forward nearly a decade later to a women's retreat, which Michelle and Candyce were leading together. The intent of the retreat was to build leadership confidence and inspire bold action in a group of working women. As the weekend progressed, it became abundantly clear that these women had one big thing in common – they were all considering a turning point in their lives but lacked the personal conviction to do it. They were using words like, "My boss thinks I would be good at …," or, "My kids really need me to …" as the signals for their life choices. They needed new internal guideposts and self-reflection to confidently go after what *they* wanted in life. Candyce decided to shift gears from the topics she had planned and share the same framework that had helped so many other leaders – *Finding Your Z*. The impact on the women was immediate and palpable. The simplicity of it and the focus on holistic decision-making provided immediate clarity and self-awareness. Together they dove into impactful and revealing conversations, which prepared them to have big conversations with the most important people in their lives.

Seeing how this framework helped at the women's retreat, Michelle tested the concept of *Finding Your Z* with a coaching client who was evaluating the next step in his career but felt paralyzed with indecision and inaction. Again, the impact was immediate. Her client quickly understood the concept and started using the language of *Finding Your Z* to explain his circumstances and choices. What he realized during that one coaching conversation became the foundation of many conversations that he decided to have with his manager, friends, and family. Soon, Michelle had taken the concept of *Finding Your Z* to the next level by developing more detailed coaching questions to support the framework. This led us to where we are today.

Throughout our careers, we have guided conversations that explore life's biggest questions. We have stood on huge stages and in front of packed classrooms talking to business leaders, networking groups, and future college graduates about how to navigate the world of work and life. We have also sat in the most intimate moments with these people, coaching them one on one, while they searched their souls for answers. It is heartbreaking to coach someone at the end of their career who has never even considered the life they wanted, because they just kept letting their career make the call. Life is so precious, and the desire people have to change their lives has never felt greater than it does right now. Observing the impact that *Finding Your Z* can have – through our workshops and coaching sessions – we decided now was the perfect time to help people on a much bigger stage, which is why we decided to write this book together.

Like most things in life, knowledge can only take you so far. You can read the directions on how to build a bookshelf; but that bookshelf isn't magically going to put itself together after you read the instructions (wouldn't it be great if it did, though)! There is a lot to learn in this book, but if all you do is read it, you won't make any meaningful changes in your life. This book contains numerous exercises and hundreds of revealing questions. It is designed to support you in having life-changing conversations with the people in your life, and help you turn your dreams into action plans. If you don't intend to do any of the exercises or convert your insights into action, we suggest putting this book back on the shelf (or remove it from your Amazon cart) because it won't help you.

Ultimately, this is a book about you. You are the third author. We invite you to reveal yourself on the pages ahead.

WE SHOULD WARN YOU.

You are going to be inspired to take action when you are done reading this book.

If you enjoy reading a book cover to cover before you get out your favorite pen or a journal to do the exercises, that's okay — we just encourage you to do the work. Dream chasing is fun, exhilarating, and rewarding but it takes effort. We hope you are ready to dig in, learn more about yourself, and make a plan to build the life of your dreams. And we are excited to be with you every step of the way.

Are you ready for the adventure of a lifetime?

66 We all have two choices: We can make a living or we can design a life. **99**

JIM ROHN

Chapter 1:

FINDING YOUR Z

FINDING YOUR Z

"Imagine your life as an alphabet, and you are trying to get to Z. If Z represents you living your ideal life, which letter are you at right now?"

This one coaching question has helped thousands of people turn confusion into clarity. It is so simple, but so powerful. The first song we learned in kindergarten is now helping adults have a breakthrough in their lives. Within moments of asking someone this question, they either realize they don't know what their Z looks like, or they blurt out a letter as if they have been waiting for years for someone to ask them about it. Somehow choosing a letter simplifies the chaos and complexity of life and orients people. It also provides a shared language and allows them to articulate their expectation gaps, ambitions, and even current level of contentment to others. This book is designed to help you use the framework of an alphabet to evaluate your life choices and ultimately, help you realize your Z.

THE POWER OF THE ALPHABET

It may seem trite to suggest that the alphabet can support the complex work of evaluating life decisions, but it is a simple framework that provides a linear path with multiple independent markers. No matter your culture, or your language, this elementary concept is understood as one with a beginning and an end. Often, when people are trying to make significant life choices, they become paralyzed by the enormity of the gap between where they are at today and where they want to be in the future. The beauty of the alphabet is that it is easy to visualize, and we have already committed it to memory. In this context, we suggest that at some point, early in life, you were at "A" and now you are parked at some other letter that represents your sense of progress. It also provides a sense of relativity in that you can measure how many letters closer to or farther away from your "Z" you are as you make new choices.

WHAT IS MY Z?

Z is the dream you are going to set at the end of your alphabet – your ideal life. *Finding your Z* is about defining success on your own terms. It is creating a vision of the life you want – a vision so clear that you are able to navigate toward it with intensity and intention. Knowing your Z allows you to operate with more confidence and show up every day knowing who you are, and where you are headed.

THE FINDING YOUR Z FRAMEWORK CONTAINS FOUR KEY ELEMENTS:

- **FINDING YOUR WHY:** In this section, we will help you get clear about your purpose, your values, and your goals. You will also create your personal definition of success.

- **FINDING YOUR WHO**: In this section, we will help you identify the most important and influential people in your life. You will also reflect on the influence they have had on you pursuing your ideal life so far.

- **FINDING YOUR WHERE**: In this section, we will help you locate your happy places in life – the destinations and lifestyle choices that will help you become the best version of yourself and feel most fully alive.

- **FINDING YOUR WHAT**: In this section we help you answer the question, "What do you want to be when you grow up?" You will also get clear about how to spend your time – professionally and personally – so you are living your best life.

To find your Z, you will look no further than inside of yourself. The answers are there if you know how to find them. That is what we are here to help you do! There are common misconceptions about Z, which are best explained by what Z is NOT.

FINDING YOUR Z IS NOT...

- **Your Retirement Plans (Necessarily):** When we ask people to imagine their Z, many individuals picture themselves in a rocking chair with gray hair. But setting your Z too many years ahead of where you are now can make it seem less urgent and tangible. It is especially hard for young people. Z doesn't have to be so far away. Instead, we encourage you to define a future point in your life – for example, an upcoming milestone birthday, or a new stage of life (like when the kids go off to school or leave the nest) – then get clear about what you want to accomplish and how you want to feel when that milestone arrives. Perhaps you want to create a Z for each year of your life. Using the framework, 26 perfectly positioned letters, allows you to customize a path for yourself toward whatever you want, in whatever time frame you choose.

If retirement really does seem like the right milestone for you, given where you are in your life, then use it.

- **It Isn't Your Dream Job:** *Finding Your Z* helps you think about your purpose in life, and what you want to accomplish in life overall. It is a much bigger question than: "What do you want to be when you grow up?" It is inviting you to envision and manifest your ideal life. Too many people have landed their dream job and lost their ideal life along the way. We will encourage you to consider how WHAT you do for a living is connected to your WHO and WHERE and WHY as well. Understanding that there are trade-offs and tensions will ensure your dream job is, well, dreamy.

- **It Isn't When You Finally Get to Be Happy:** Your Z is not a final destination, and it can be ever-changing. Throughout life, you will have new experiences and learnings, and as a result, your Z will change over time. The joy is in the journey. Don't wait to feel happy – this isn't about suffering and striving until you reach the end of your life or your alphabet. You can, and should, feel happy and fulfilled at every letter. Happiness is a choice and being happy does not mean you are done growing and striving.

Deciding what your Z is can feel overwhelming. The book you are holding was created to help people who are struggling with that very question. If you can't describe your Z right now, that's normal. We should warn you that the *Finding Your Z* toolkit does *not* involve completing statistical assessments that result in a computer printout with a diagnosis of what your Z is or where you land in the alphabet today. For some of you that is good news, and some of you may want your money back. Okay – don't panic. We will break it down to show you how it works.

Jonathan's Story

Every time we teach the *Finding Your Z* concept, we ask people to yell out the letter that represents where they are at in life right now. Only once has someone yelled out "Z." It was a young man who happened to be sitting right in the front of the room. When Candyce turned to locate the voice, she was surprised to see that it came from a young man who was about 25 years old.

She stopped dead in her tracks, and asked him, "Really? You are at the letter Z right now?"

"Yep," he said smiling and nodding voraciously. Okay … she got curious.

"Well good for you! But tell me why you think are you at Z?"

He continued, undeterred, "Well, I am making more money than I ever thought I would at my age, I live in a cool apartment with my best friends, I have a smoking-hot girlfriend, and I go out nearly every night. We are having the time of our lives! Honestly, I don't think it's going to get better than this for me."

The entire class burst into laughter and applauded his fabulous life.

Candyce said, "Well, you might be right. That really might be as good as it gets."

For a moment Candyce, and everyone else in the class, considered that the whole notion of *Finding Your Z* was baloney. Maybe we all had experienced our "Z" a long time ago and had missed it.

But then Candyce remembered something really important … being happy doesn't mean you're done. You don't "tap-out" and stop dreaming just because you are feeling fortunate for the life you have now. Life is a wild ride with lots of twists and turns. Road conditions are changing constantly! This young man wasn't *done*, he was just getting started!

So she said to him, "I think it's great that you are so happy right now. Clearly you have made some smart decisions and are learning what really matters to you in life. But if I come find you in 10 years and you're still partying every single night, working at the same job, living in the same apartment with your buddies, and you have the same girlfriend – who is probably a little less hot – will you still be at Z?"

"No, that would be depressing," he acknowledged with a laugh.

"Exactly! So being happy right now doesn't mean you are finished. It just means you are doing it right! When it comes time for you to evaluate new careers, roommates, or lifestyles, you should make thoughtful choices that feel like progress. I hope you continue to be just as happy as you are now for the rest of your life. And I hope enjoy every letter along the way."

Jonathan's story is a great example of the evolving nature of Z and the importance of defining success for yourself as your life and circumstances change. He was incredibly happy where he was at in life, so the next opportunity that came his way would have to be pretty compelling. Let's say Jonathan was actually at "G" right now and somebody offered him a job in Boston. Should he move to Boston and leave his friends and their apartment? What does he value more than that – Money? Status? Growth? If Jonathan wants to stay as happy he is at "G," moving to Boston needs to have a purpose and provide more of something he really cares about. Otherwise, he could accidentally move backward in his alphabet.

Candyce encouraged Jonathan to think about the journey of *Finding Your Z* as a long road trip through the alphabet instead of a final destination. Life handed him a set of keys but it is up to him where he goes, and how much he will continue to enjoy the ride.

❝ Create the highest grandest vision possible for your life, because you become what you believe. **❞**

OPRAH WINFREY

Using This Book

Throughout this book, you will be presented with opportunities for reflection and asked to apply the concepts we share to your own life using guided tools and exercises. It is one thing to read a book, it is quite another to *use* it. We have designed this book to be used, not just read. Let it be your journal and an ongoing GPS for your life. Let it become the dog-eared reference for your "Heck Yes" or "Heck No" responses when life throws options your way. We hope each page encourages you to find your Z and define your success.

We decided to use the metaphor of taking a "road trip" when we talk about the journey of realizing your ideal life. Using this metaphor, we explore each of the four elements of *Finding Your Z – Finding Your WHY, Finding Your WHO, Finding Your WHERE,* and *Finding Your WHAT* – and suggest how you can fuel your journey and overcome the roadblocks that get people stuck along the way. We will also examine the biggest obstacle people need to overcome – the voice in their head, or their inner critic. We call this voice *Your Backseat Driver.*

Along the way you will see a few icons appear that are designed to help you navigate the book and easily locate the most important stops on your route.

This icon indicates that it is time to take out your pen and do some reflection.

This icon indicates that some powerful coaching questions are nearby. We think you should pull over and look at them.

Occasionally we will give you the option of going farther into an exercise to gain even more clarity and awareness. This icon indicates an optional, but valuable, detour.

USING THE ALPHABET

Finding Your Z is a great conversation starter because people can quickly understand the concept and identify their life with a letter. You should try it! Choose someone in your life and ask them our coaching question: **"Imagine your life as an alphabet, and you are trying to get to Z. If Z represents you living your ideal life, which letter are you at right now?"**

You will see how amazing this simple question is at unlocking insights and helping people open up. You might hear them say things like, "I feel like I just moved backward in life and I'm at the letter C again because …," or, "I feel like I am near the end of the alphabet, like around the letter V." There is no right answer to this question – people can't guess the wrong letter. It is a gut check, an inner knowing, that senses where we are – at the beginning, middle, or closer to the end of the alphabet, as it relates to our ideal life.

In our experience, nearly everyone picks a letter other than Z, because people sense that progress is always available to them. Right now, you are somewhere along the path to Z as well. You don't have to leap to Z from where you are because the framework provides many mile markers. Selecting a letter allows you to consider, "What is one decision or one action I could take that would get me a letter closer to Z?" You don't have to worry about figuring out all of the steps – you only need to make progress. Don't be concerned about the gap between where you are and Z – you only need to think about what might get you to the next letter. In fact, sometimes making progress can actually take you backward in the alphabet for a period of time. You might make a decision that takes you back to "H" (like going back to school or learning a new trade) because you know it will eventually leapfrog you to "P" and provide the lifestyle you want.

Let's put the alphabet to work using your real life. Consider a life decision you may be facing right now – for example, moving houses, accepting a new job, having more children, spending money on a renovation project, or selecting the right school. Now use the alphabet to visualize the choices you are facing and how they might relate to your current letter and your Z.

EXERCISE 1:
Mapping Your Z

During our coaching sessions, we will often take out a map of the alphabet and use it to help people evaluate their life decisions. In this exercise, you will be asked to evaluate a life decision using the alphabet.

Here's an example to show you how this works:

Corey sensed she was currently at the letter "G" in her life – still near the beginning of her career. She had been offered a promotion but wasn't sure if she should take it. We got out our alphabet map and circled the letter "G." Then we asked, "Which letter would this new role take you to?" Corey thought about it for a minute and answered, "J." She knew it would be a small step back in her personal life (longer workdays, less free time) but it would feel like progress in terms of her salary and what she wanted to learn. When we asked how it would feel to turn it down, Corey said that it would likely result in her being stuck at "G" for a few more years. Then she said, "Saying no actually makes my current job feel like a step backwards" So we marked Option 2 (Turning it Down) as moving to the letter "E." Comparing these options visually made her feel clear and confident about what she wanted to do. She said yes and accepted the promotion.

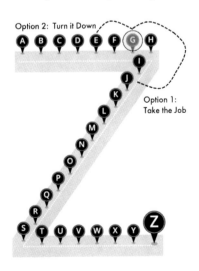

Option 2: Turn it Down

Option 1:
Take the Job

Now it is your turn! Use the following page to evaluate a life decision you are wrestling with. It doesn't have to be a professional decision – it could be getting married, moving, making an investment, having children, or whatever else you are trying to thoughtfully decide. You will then use the alphabet to evaluate your options and consider why they feel like a move forward or a move backwards in your life.

STEP 1: Circle the letter that represents where you are at in the alphabet right now.

STEP 2: Consider a choice you are wrestling with in your life. Use the alphabet to show where two different options could take you. Circle the letter that represents how each option moves you forward or backward on the alphabet.

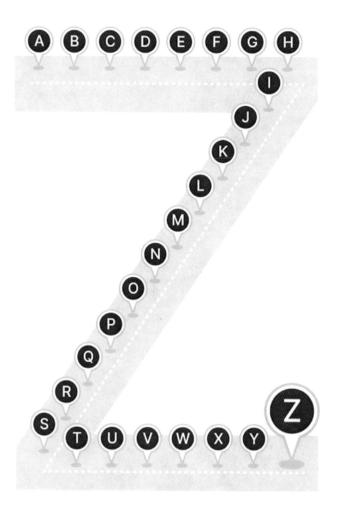

My Current Letter: _____

What is a choice you are struggling to make at this point in your life?

_____

_____

OPTION 1 **moves you to the Letter_____**

OPTION 2 **moves you to the Letter_____**

What are you realizing? Which option will ultimately get you closer to your Z? _____

_____

NOTE: The "criteria" you just used to evaluate these life decisions are indicators of your values! More on that in the Chapter "Finding Your WHY"!

The key to using the alphabet is to help you make life choices more *intentionally*. We often make choices because they are easy or comfortable or convenient – it is the path of least resistance. These choices may not be part of an overall vision or a plan for where you want to go. Choices thoughtfully considered in isolation minimize the broader context and impact. For example, a person in our life recently quit their job without lining up another job. One of their children was struggling at school and needed more time and attention. Quitting did not acknowledge the financial realities that they faced or the fulfillment they found in their work. In hindsight, this individual wished they had spoken with their boss about what was happening and asked for a sabbatical or pursued freelance work before resigning.

It can be really enticing to dream – to make vision boards, set goals, or create a movie in our minds about how life can be. All of those things are inspiring, wonderful, and important. However, a dream is only a dream. Unless you are taking *intentional action* those dreams remain just that. The *Finding Your Z* framework helps you to get clear on all aspects of your ideal life and define the actions that will get you closer to Z – one letter at a time.

EXERCISE 2:
Checking Your Gauges

We are all at different stages of clarity when it comes to imagining our ideal life. Let's break down each element of *Finding Your Z* using a quick exercise called "Check the Gauges." This exercise will invite you to consider your current level of clarity (or confusion) in each element of the *Finding Your Z* framework. To complete it, you will simply read the description of each gauge on the following pages and mark your personal level of clarity in that area. This will help you determine which sections to focus on in the book.

MY WHY

Unclear   Clear

I know **WHY** I make the decisions I do. I can confidently articulate what matters most to me – including my values, my goals, and my definition of success.

MY WHO

Unclear   Clear

I know **WHO** the most important people are in my life and intentionally include them in my journey. I know how to manage the influence they have on my decisions.

MY WHERE

Unclear   Clear

I know **WHERE** my happy place is. I intentionally navigate my life towards these activities and destinations.

MY WHAT

Unclear   Clear

I know **WHAT** I should spend my time doing and what I should not spend my time doing. I can clearly articulate my professional "sweet spot" to others.

OVERVIEW OF FINDING YOUR **WHY**

This section of the book will help you craft your personal definition of success and examine your purpose and values in life. It enables you to confidently articulate what matters most to you, what motivates you, and recalibrates your "internal GPS" so you can make more deliberate decisions in the future.

HOW CLEAR ARE YOU ABOUT YOUR WHY?

I know WHY I make the decisions I do. I can clearly and confidently articulate what matters most to me – including my values, my goals, and my personal definition of success.

Draw a line that indicates your current level of clarity in Finding Your WHY.

UNCLEAR   **CLEAR**

Why do you feel that way?_____

_____

_____

OVERVIEW OF FINDING YOUR **WHO**

This section will help you identify the most important people in your life and intentionally consider how much influence they have over your dreams. It encourages you to be mindful about who you are sharing your life with, and the power they have over you reaching your Z. Life can feel meaningful or meaningless when certain people are by your side.

HOW CLEAR ARE YOU ABOUT YOUR WHO?

I know WHO the most important people are in my life and intentionally include them in my journey. I know how to manage the influence they have on my decisions.

Draw a line that indicates your current level of clarity in Finding Your WHO.

UNCLEAR   **CLEAR**

Why do you feel that way?_____

_____

_____

OVERVIEW OF FINDING YOUR **WHERE**

This section will help you identify your happy place and the lifestyle you want. It encourages you to navigate toward the destinations and experiences that make you feel most like yourself. WHERE has been found to have a bigger impact on your happiness than almost any other variable. The lifestyle you have is a significant indicator of whether or not you feel fulfilled in life.

HOW CLEAR ARE YOU ABOUT YOUR WHERE?

I know WHERE my happy place is and I am intentionally navigating my life toward specific experiences and destinations.

Draw a line that indicates your current level of clarity in Finding Your WHERE.

UNCLEAR   **CLEAR**

Why do you feel that way?_____

_____

_____

OVERVIEW OF FINDING YOUR **WHAT**

This section helps you define your professional "sweet spot." It also helps you evaluate the professions and interests that you should invest your time in pursuing because you are uniquely capable of thriving in those roles or environments.

HOW CLEAR ARE YOU ABOUT YOUR WHAT?

I know WHAT I should spend my time doing and what I should not spend my time doing. I can clearly articulate my professional "sweet spot" to others.

Draw a line that indicates your current level of clarity in Finding Your WHAT.

UNCLEAR   CLEAR

Why do you feel that way?_____

_____

_____

We will revisit these gauges at the end of each chapter to see if your clarity has shifted. Notice where you currently have the most clarity and where you have the least. Notice where you feel furthest ahead or behind in your life.

Included in each chapter are enlightening exercises and thought-provoking questions that will help you twist life's lenses into focus so you are able to get a better understanding of what your Z might be. Hopefully, we will move all of those needles closer to "CLEAR" by the end of this book!

In addition to exploring the four elements of Z, you will also have an opportunity to:

- **Take Your Driver's Test:** Consider different types of travelers on the road of life and identify what type of driver you might be. This section helps you consider the habit loops and mindsets you will need to confront if you want to reach your Z.

- **Meet Your Backseat Driver:** Dream chasing is a mental game as much as it is an act of physical endurance. In this section, we will examine the impact of having an active inner critic (which we call *Your Backseat Driver*) and teach you how to manage or even silence it.

- **Fuel Your Journey:** Do you have the proper "fuel" you need to sustain your journey to Z? Gain valuable insights on the importance of managing your time, money, and well-being if you want to reach your goals. Explore the role of grit and resilience, as well as the power of support systems, to help you reach your destination.

- **Hear Stories from the Road:** Enjoy real-life stories throughout the book of people who got stuck, made mistakes, and took unexpected detours in their lives. Learn how they dealt with failure and overcame challenges in pursuit of their dreams.

- **And Get in the Driver's Seat:** This section will help you pull it all together and create a roadmap for realizing your ideal life.

So that's the idea. After decades of teaching and coaching leaders at top companies, we know this seemingly simple concept is one of the most powerful things we have ever shared. People have paid us thousands of dollars to ask them these questions, but now we are sharing them with YOU with the hope that they will help you enjoy a more fulfilling life.

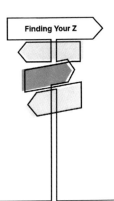

This book can be truly life changing if you are willing to do the work. It is time to get back in the driver's seat of your life.

Let's go find your Z!

Fred's Story

Candyce's family shares this personal story to demonstrate how you can be at different letters in different aspects of your life. It is a story about someone who accidently made a trade-off that was derailing his happiness, and how the alphabet brought him back.

This story belongs to her husband Fred. As you might imagine, being married to somebody like Candyce means you find yourself in a lot of impromptu coaching or calibration conversations. It was during one of those conversations that Fred shared that he'd been reflecting on his alphabet, and where he wanted to be, and he had an epiphany. For the past three years he had been in a new "stretch assignment" at work that required him to travel extensively, all over the world, and work long hours. As a result, Candyce and their daughters had established life rhythms and pastimes that didn't include him.

He shared, "I feel pretty satisfied with the letter I'm at in my professional life as that is something I've put a lot of time and energy into. But if I tell you which letter I feel like I'm at in my personal life, it would be a very different answer."

He continued by saying, "I'm falling behind in our family. So I've decided that if my company asks me to take on a bigger role, or a project that requires me to travel like I am now, I'm going to pass. I want to catch up on my alphabet at home."

It was an emotional conversation, but he was clear and convicted. The sentence Candyce remembers most was when Fred said, "I've only got a few years left with our girls before they graduate, and I want to get to Z as their dad before they leave."

To his credit, he absolutely did. He ended up accepting a new role at a new company and is now the primary chef in the family and far more involved in his children's lives. His days are more balanced, and he is far happier. Their daughters love it too.

You can make the alphabet your own. Use the framework however you need to, and use it as a way to have conversations with your spouse, your kids, your boss, or your friends. Let it help you connect with others as you navigate this crazy little thing called life together.

Chapter 2:

YOUR DRIVER'S TEST

Cathy's Story

Cathy loved a roadtrip. The hours spent staring out the windshield were not wasted on her. It gave her mind time to process and reflect on things – something her "real life" rarely allowed her to do. Her daughter recently started college at the University of Chicago so when she noticed her calendar for the weekend looked open, she decided to jump in her car and surprise her daughter at school.

Cathy lives in Minnesota and it was November. It did not dawn on her that the weather might be a problem until it started snowing and the freeway began to disappear under her headlights. Undeterred, she pressed on, turning up the radio and singing along at the top of her voice.

She was excited to see her daughter's face when she arrived in a few hours. She imagined the time they would spend shopping together, the nice dinners they'd enjoy in her favorite foodie city, and how great it would be to meet all her new friends. She had missed her daughter so much during the past few months, so even though Thanksgiving was just around the corner, it was too far away for her to wait.

Within the hour, the road conditions deteriorated and Cathy realized that she would be sleeping somewhere other than Chicago that night. She pulled into a small town to find a hotel room for the night. The first three hotels she went to were already full of travelers, but she managed to find a motel on the edge of town. She fell asleep in her clothes, the smell of cigarette smoke mixed with raw onions surrounding her, overly eager to get back on the road the next day.

The next morning the sun was shining bright – an omen of the great day ahead she thought! As she pulled up to her daughter's dormitory she decided to call her.

"Hey Honey! What are you up to today?"

"Oh, I went home with one of my friends to meet her family and work on a project for school."

Cathy's heart sunk. Her dream weekend poofed away. "Where does your friend live?"

"In Northern Wisconsin."

"Oh, that's too bad. Because I'm at your dorm right now and was planning to surprise you for the weekend."

Her daughter went quiet and then said, "I'm so sorry Mom. I wish you'd let me know what you were planning."

Cathy hung up frustrated and berating herself for not being more planful.

When Cathy shared this story on her next coaching call we used it as an example of how she might be approaching other decisions in her life. Cathy is someone that appreciates spontaenity and adventure. She is incredibly talented but has navigated most of her career unintentionally. People have tapped her on the shoulder and asked her to take the jobs they thought she would be great at. She accepted many of these on the spot without consulting her family first – even though more than three of those opportunities required the family to move to a new state! Now she was a senior leader with a Fortune 100 company but struggling personally. She was an overworked, burned-out, deeply unfullfilled empty nester. She needed a plan to get her life back on track. But seeing the parallels in how she'd approached the weekend roadtrip to Chicago helped open her up to the idea that there was another way to navigate this next phase of her life. Deciding to go to Chicago was all about her and what she wanted – to slow down and enjoy a fun weekend in Chicago eating great food, and seeing the daughter she missed. It was time for her to stop wandering and create a plan that led to more personal fullfilment – and she wanted to share that plan with the people she loves.

PREPARING FOR YOUR DRIVER'S TEST

Have you ever heard someone say, "How you do anything is how you do everything"? It means that your tendencies in one area of your life also manifest themselves in other areas of your life. Consider how your preference for a certain pace of life, your ability to connect with people (or not), or your tendency to be critical or sarcastic shows up both at work and at home. The point is, we have one brain and we take it everywhere. Your brain is wired to process information in a very specific way. It has been shaped uniquely by your life experiences and the most challenging events you have survived. When bad things happen you have been programmed to react in a way that the brain believes will keep you safe mentally and physically. When you think you are in danger, chemicals are released into your bloodstream (adrenaline and cortisol) which stimulate a reaction. People react to these life events in predictable patterns. Examining your patterns is a valuable investment in your personal growth.

Have you ever been in a job interview where they ask you, "Tell me about a time when you …blah, blah, blah?" Do you know why they ask that question? It's because past behavior is the best predictor of future behavior. Meaning – how you react in a certain circumstance will likely be replicated in future, similar circumstances. This is particularly true when situations are perceived as stressful, uncomfortable, or new.

This chapter invites you to consider how you are wired and how you might react to the unknown adversity that inevitably appears on your journey to Z. You will be asked to think about your past and consider how it might impact your future. This can be a very eye-opening experience! Some people realize that the reason they don't set goals, take chances, or trust themselves is directly related to the mindsets they have cultivated since childhood and the things they believe are absolute truths about themselves and others. So it is time to look in the mirror.

Let's get your brain warmed up to this idea with an exercise we call: "My Journey to Now."

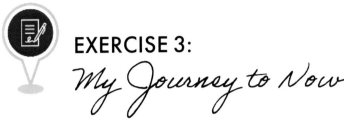

EXERCISE 3:
My Journey to Now

Reflect on your life up to this point and finish each of the sentences below:

Growing up, I was raised to believe that the most important things in life were:

Because of this, my definition of success has been:

Which is why, on a typical day, you will find me:

Overall, I would describe my life as:

Sometimes I worry that my life is not _____ enough.

I long to spend more time:

And spend less time:

If I represented my life as a road sign, my sign would be...

WHAT'S YOUR SIGN?

OR DRAW YOUR OWN SIGN ABOVE

Nice work! What you just wrote provides some important insights for the exercises that follow.

WHAT KIND OF DRIVER ARE YOU?

We are going to introduce you to a few personas we have encountered on the road of life. We have lovingly characterized each of them using our road trip analogy and the descriptions of different drivers. As you read through these Driver personas, ask yourself if you recognize any of them. **Which type of driver are you? Do you see these characteristics in other people in your life? How do you see these tendencies influencing your life decisions?**

As you read these descriptions, you might identify with a couple of the Driver personas or you might choose to take this analogy and create your own! Maybe you will think, "I'm actually an Uber Driver and let me tell you why." Have fun with it! The most important thing is for you to think about your current mindsets and tendencies, and how these might be impacting the way you navigate your life right now.

TYPES OF DRIVERS

If you are a Speed Demon, you are out there accomplishing life. You are going 100 miles an hour with intense focus on pursuing your goals but tend to miss all the scenery along the way. You enjoy life in the fast lane and may have very little regard for the other drivers on the road. It is all about the finish line for you – checkmarks, milestones, levels, and titles. You tend to reach whatever goals you set for yourself and are competitive with other drivers, comparing yourself to them as you cruise on by.

CAUTION: The finish line you are gunning for may feel meaningless once you reach it. Speed Demons rarely ask themselves about their WHY, WHO, or WHERE because they are so focused on their WHAT. If you are a classic overachiever and aren't careful, you could find yourself all alone in your shiny sports car having accomplished society's version of success instead of your own.

A SPEED DEMON IS OFTEN LACKING

- Purpose/Meaning

- Balance (Prone to Burnout)

- Deep Personal Connections with Others

- Self-Awareness

Questions for a Speed Demon to Consider

- *How do you define success?*

- *Why does this goal matter to you?*

- *What are you longing to have more of in your life? What do you want less of?*

- *What is depleting your energy?*

- *Why do you work?*

- *What percentage of your daily energy is invested in creating a better professional life? What percentage is invested in creating a better personal life?*

- *What brings you a sense of fulfillment?*

- *Where do your work and home life intersect? Where does it crash?*

- *Who are the most important people in your life? Who do you spend the most time with?*

- *At the end of your life, what do you want people to say about you?*

If you are a Wanderer, you might feel anxious reading this book as you just want to go with the flow and be in the moment. You like to live free of constraints and do whatever feels good or right at the time. You value spontaneity and the ability to be opportunistic. Wanderers tend to gradually isolate themselves from others because they struggle to commit to anything they sense is permanent. Wanderers aren't lazy, they are directionless.

CAUTION: If you aren't careful you might use up all of your fuel not getting to where you hoped you would go. You might look back on your life and realize that you missed opportunities to make intentional decisions that would have put you on the path you deeply desired.

WANDERERS ARE OFTEN LACKING

- Focus

- Clarity

- A Sense of Urgency

- Appreciation for Planning their Future

- Desire to Reflect on Past Mistakes

Questions for a Wanderer to Consider

- *What are your priorities at this point in your life (values, etc)?*

- *How are you approaching decision making at this point in your life?*

- *Imagine your future-self giving you advice. What would they want you to start doing now so you could be happier later?*

- *What gets in the way of you accomplishing your goals or being happier?*

- *What are the non-negotiables in your life?*

- *What is a mistake you have learned the hard way and how are you applying those lessons in your life right now?*

If you are a White Knuckler, when given the chance to dream, or take a different path, your shoulders might become tense and you might begin to death-grip the steering wheel. You have a bad case of the *Yeah-Buts*. "Yeah, but do you know what would happen if I did that? Yeah, but if I tried that I'd probably run off the road. Yeah, but this is Reason 249 why that won't work for me." You articulate those fears to rationalize not taking action. Instead, you just keep driving on the road you know because taking risks or exploring a road less traveled scares you to death. Failure is not an option.

There is also a fear of leaving your comfort zone.

 CAUTION: White Knucklers often keep themselves safe by pulling off to the side of the road before they reach their Z and become really annoyed by (jealous of) the Speed Demons passing them by.

WHITE KNUCKLERS OFTEN LACK

- Risk Tolerance

- Growth Mindset

- Inspiration / Passion

- Self-Confidence

Questions for a White Knuckler to Consider

- *When was the last time you made a spontaneous decision? What happened?*

- *When did you learn that failing was unforgivable?*

- *What is an experience that made you uncomfortable? What did you learn from that experience?*

- *Consider a decision you are currently contemplating. What is at stake for you by making this decision? What is at stake if you don't make this decision?*

- *What could you lose that matters to you? How could you mitigate those losses?*

- *What information do you need to confidently make this decision?*

- *What are you risking by doing nothing?*

If you are a Passenger, you allow other people to be in the driver's seat of YOUR life. You wait for others to decide where you are going and what you are going to do next. You might have a "can do" career right now – a career shaped by the things you "can do" versus the things you "want to do." You spend years of your life in jobs you don't like because you don't want to disappoint your family or your boss or your team. Your desire to be helpful or support other people's needs sabotages your own happiness.

CAUTION: You might be putting everybody else's Z ahead of your own – your kids, your spouse, your friends, even strangers. As everyone else inches closer to their Z, yours may get further and further away. This builds resentment in your relationships and leads to trouble down the road.

PASSENGERS OFTEN LACK

- Self-Confidence

- Self-Awareness

- Conviction

- Appreciation for What They are Missing Out On

Questions for a Passengers to Consider

- *What do YOU want?*

- *When you are trying to make a decision, who do you involve and why?*

- *What would you do if no one else could have an opinion about it?*

- *Imagine three different realities. Which one makes you feel most excited?*

- *Who are the most influential people in your life? To what extent are they helping you live your ideal life?*

- *Imagine telling someone important in your life what you really want to do. What fears or anxieties does this cause for you?*

Oh, Commuters — you break our hearts! You might be a Commuter if you feel like it is impossible for you to be doing anything other than what you are doing right now. You believe your deep expertise, circumstances, or educational background prevent any new life choices — maybe you went to medical school, own your parents' farm, or are one of the few people in the world who can do what you do. We meet people that were told to get a job in technology because they liked video games in high school. Now, after 10 years of working as a computer programmer, they believe they will never be qualified for anything else — and they HATE programming! They chose to ignore every Exit Ramp they come across except the one that leads them directly to the life they have been sentenced to.

CAUTION: If you are living your life on autopilot, or it hurt to read this description, start talking to people about it. This type of driver is prone to depression. If you don't get your swagger back soon, you could miss this one precious life you have been given.

COMMUTERS OFTEN LACK:

- The Vision of a Different Life

- Joy / Fun

- Encouragement

- Perceived Freedom to Explore Options

Questions for a Commuter to Consider

- *When you were young, what did you dream of growing up to be?*

- *What are the goals you have for your life at this point?*

- *To what extent are you able to realize your goals if you continue on your current path?*

- *What would an abundant life look like for you? What would you have more of or less of than you have now?*

- *If you knew you would be successful, what would you try?*

- *Knowing what you know now, what do you wish you had gone to school for?*

- *What is a good first step if you wanted to move towards this new job/life?*

- *What is a safe experiment you could run?*

- *How do you feel imagining this new life?*

Driving Instructors know the rules of the road. You check all of your mirrors before making any big moves and are mindful of your passengers and other driver's safety when switching lanes. You have spent a significant amount of time behind the wheel, so your instincts are sharp. You pay attention to changing road conditions and are able to respond and adjust quickly. In fact, you are so confident in how to navigate life, that you may offer to help other people drive as well.

Because you are so aware, you tend to follow the letter of the law and not take any chances. You play it safe because you want to get to your desired destination. It may feel "right" or "responsible" to stick with the route highlighted on the map instead of taking the road less traveled.

CAUTION: You are doing a lot of things right but keep being a learner and don't rely too much on your rearview mirror. Remain curious about your journey and be willing to chart new courses as needed.

DRIVING INSTRUCTORS OFTEN LACK

- Spontaneity

- Trying New Things

- Allowing People to Have Their Own Experiences

Questions for a Driving Instructor to Consider

- *How do you handle situations that are new or unpredictable?*

- *When was the last time you made a choice for the benefit of yourself versus for others?*

- *When was the last time you took a chance and did the irresponsible thing? How did it make you feel?*

- *How do you feel when others in your life don't follow the rules? How does that affect your happiness?*

EXERCISE 4:

Reflecting on Your Driver's Test

Do you recognize yourself in any of these personas? If none of them holds true for you, describe the type of driver you are:

What type of Driver are you? _____

Describe the characteristics of this Driver:

GO FURTHER!

OK, hopefully that revealed some important insights for you. Let's pull over and consider how your tendencies as a Driver could impact your ability to realize an ideal life.

How does being this type of Driver impact your life?

What kind of driver do you want to be?

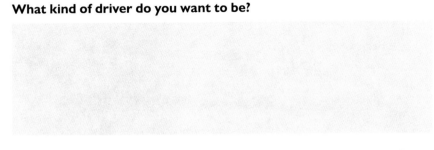

How would that change how you approach your life and choices?

Once you identify the type of Driver you are, and understand the impact it may be having on your life, what's next? The answer is…the rest of this book! Keep going! You are in the "Awareness" stage right now – next is "Growth!" The remaining chapters explore new questions and exercises that will challenge your mindsets and help you develop the vision, confidence, and motivation you will need to chase your dreams.

Let's Go Find Your WHY!

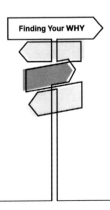

Chapter 3:

FINDING YOUR WHY

FINDING YOUR WHY
Questions to Explore

- *What is the impact I want to make in the world?*

- *What matters most to me? What are my values?*

- *What is my personal definition of success?*

- *What are the goals I want to set for myself to have a more meaningful life?*

These are hefty questions that often require deeper thinking and time to digest. We'll spend the next several pages breaking down each question and invite you to complete Reflection Exercises that will help you realize your WHY.

Andy's Story

Andy's story is a powerful example of how important it is to find your WHY if you want to find your Z. Andy was in the prime of his life – he had a successful career at a Fortune 50 company, a loving marriage, and three beautiful children – then he received the diagnosis that changed everything for him and his family: Stage 4 Cancer.

The amazing thing about Andy is, rather than viewing the diagnosis as a death sentence, he and his wife Michael chose to make cancer their teacher – they began seeking the "gifts of cancer" and got clarity about what was most important to them in life. Cancer helped them find their WHY and they prayed that their fight would not be over before cancer taught them everything they needed to learn.

Andy tells his story this way: "I got over 50 different and amazing gifts from cancer. One of the biggest gifts is this intense, immediate grounding of what's important in my life. I've got to be a daddy, that's a big one. I've got to be a coach. I've got to keep doing music. And I've got to keep being the best husband I can be for Michael – that's it!"

Andy's wife Michael elaborates further about the impact cancer had on their Z as a couple and as a family, "Cancer asks you if you are present. If your Z doesn't matter today, if it doesn't affect the decisions you are making today, you are missing something."

Andy adds, "If I could put that in terms for people who may not have gone through cancer, don't hesitate to do those things that you know in your heart of hearts, in your soul, in your body, in your bones that are super important to you. It doesn't need to be your whole life, it doesn't need to be all of your time, but make time for those things that you know are important to you."

Andy, along with his doctors, continue to routinely monitor his health. While his cancer journey has its ups and downs, he always finds a way to appreciate the beauty in life and recognizes the evidence of miracles that continuously appear. Since being diagnosed with cancer, he has gone on to become a certified executive coach, has recorded an album of his original music, is writing a book with his wife Michael entitled *The Gifts of Cancer*, and continues to prioritize his roles as a husband and a daddy.

Watch Andy & Michael's Story

FINDING YOUR WHY

Now, more than ever, people are seeking meaning and purpose in their life. This chapter will help you reveal what yours could be.

Think about your WHY as your internal GPS. It is the "True North" navigation system that you filter every decision through. Your navigation system is uniquely programmed because of the experiences you have had and what you have learned in your lifetime. Your "True North" is different than your parents. It is different than your friends or loved ones. It is why when faced with a decision you possess an inner knowing of what you should do – think of it as a green-light or red-light reaction. A green-light reaction is when you say, "I want to keep moving towards that. That feels right for me. I want more of that in my life."

Or maybe you have a red-light reaction. As you imagine yourself doing it, you are filled with a sense of dread, hesitation, or heaviness. You might think, "Geez, something just feels off about this to me." That internal awareness or gut-check moment matters when it comes to *Finding Your WHY*. Successful people are tuned into the sensation of moving toward things that make them feel happier – a relationship, a career, or even a lifestyle – and away from things that deplete them.

Whenever you feel your green or red lights coming on, pay attention to WHY.

NOTE: You can absolutely choose to ignore these default reactions. You can go against them. It's no different than what we do when we ignore the navigation system in our car – when we hear the nagging voice saying, "You have left the planned route! Please proceed to the highlighted route!" That navigation system was expertly programmed to identify the most efficient path to get you where you want to go.

However, many people decide that they know better, or listen to other people in the car who suggest there is a better way. As a result, they ignore the promptings and explore other routes believing that they will reach their destination faster. How many times has that worked out for you? How many times have you listened to your passenger's advice and wished you had just done what the nagging voice told you to do in the first place?

Your WHY or "inner knowing" is that nagging voice. It senses the right thing to do, but you may not be tuned into it or trust it yet. The more tuned in you are to your own internal GPS, your WHY, the more confidently you will start to navigate the life decisions you face on your journey to Z. This chapter is designed to help you do just that.

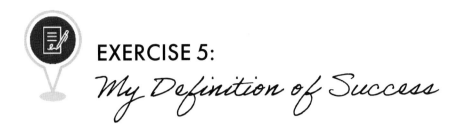

EXERCISE 5:
My Definition of Success

Let's get curious about your current definition of success.

Close your eyes and envision yourself at Z. You are successful and fulfilled.

- *What do you look like in this vision?*

- *What have you spent your lifetime time doing?*

- *Where do you live?*

- *Who else is in your life?*

The entire image may not be very clear at first but notice any specific elements of the image that *DO* feel clear to you. If you can't quite fully envision your Z, imagine where you might be a few years from now. It's okay if you don't have a fully developed vision just yet — just look for some clues to get you started!

Capture your personal definition of success below.

_____

_____

_____

DEFINING SUCCESS FOR YOURSELF

The cultural messages we have received about what success looks like are so strong that if you ask the average American to define it, their language is eerily similar. You should go to college, get a good job, get married, have kids, buy a house, go on nice vacations, drive nice cars, be respected in your community, etc. But what if you don't personally value any of those things? Most of us know people who have those things and recognize that they are still deeply unhappy. That narrow path is not the path everyone should follow. Certain accomplishments will never feel fulfilling, while other less conventional choices might feel deeply meaningful. Your unique upbringing and experiences have shaped what the right choices might be for you – for example, spending time being creative or going on mountain climbing adventures might bring YOU more joy than a new car or bigger job.

Speaking of big jobs, as executive coaches we are often hired to work with C-suite leaders – meaning CEOs, CFOs, COOs – that are at the pinnacle of their careers. They have worked tirelessly to reach these levels in their organizations and now feel stuck or lost as they face retirement. When we sit down with them, we are armed with important questions that we have learned unlock deeper insights and self-awareness. These are the same questions we will be asking you!

Questions like:

- *What is your personal definition of success?*
- *What criteria do you use to make important life decisions?*
- *What do you want more of in your life?*
- *What do you want less of in your life?*

In our experience, coaching a CEO or a multimillionaire is often a surprising conversation. We have met with far too many who have everything the world would define as symbols of success but see their lives as a failed test. Somehow they lost what mattered most while pursuing something the world told them mattered. It is hard to see people suffer like that! Talking to people in their 50s and 60s who say, "I wish I could start over, I've wasted my life," is one of the biggest reasons we wrote this book.

We want to help people like you examine their WHY earlier in life – realizing your motivation, sources of happiness, and purpose will help you more fully enjoy your life. This is the most meaningful and impactful work we get to do in the world and we are grateful to be doing it for you.

"One should not search for an abstract meaning of life. Everyone has their own specific vocation or mission in life to carry out – a concrete assignment which demands fulfillment. You cannot be replaced, nor can your life be repeated. **"**

VIKTOR FRANKL,
MAN'S SEARCH FOR MEANING

EXERCISE 6:
My 80th Birthday Party

Another way to gain clarity about your life's purpose, or your WHY, is called "Futurecasting." Futurecasting involves imagining a time much later in your life and figuratively looking back at what you had to do to arrive where you wanted to be. In *Seven Habits of Highly Effective People*, author Stephen Covey suggests that you think about your own funeral and imagine what people would say in your eulogy. Imagining your funeral can be a bit depressing, so instead we suggest imagining that you are celebrating your 80th birthday with a huge party where everyone important in your life is there — from all parts of your life — friends, family, colleagues, neighbors, etc. At a party like that you are surrounded by people who know you well. They have seen how you made decisions and how you prioritized your time, money, and energy.

In these moments, people often grab a microphone and stand up to talk about the person they are celebrating. These speeches become a playback movie of their life. It is a reflection on the manifestation of whatever successes they've enjoyed in their lifetime and their most meaningful contributions. It's a live testimonial about the impact they've had on people's lives. In this exercise we invite you to imagine what you WANT people to say about you and your life in such a moment.

Imagine you are at your 80th birthday party and somebody you really care about, someone you've spent a good amount of your life with, stands up and grabs the microphone. Who would you want to raise a glass and toast you? Who are the people you want sitting beside you on this important day? As they start delivering their toast to you, what would you want them to say about you? How would they describe you? What positive qualities will they say you possess? What impact would they say you have had on their life? What would they say is the most important thing they've learned from you? How will the words they say confirm that you've lived a successful, fulfilling life — that you reached your potential? What did you end up doing with this one precious life you had?

Take a moment and write the toast you want offered at your 80th birthday party.

WHO DO YOU WANT TO DELIVER THIS TOAST? _____

WHAT DO YOU WANT THEM TO SAY? *Write the toast here:*

Re-read the toast you just wrote down because within it may be your true **Personal Success Statement**. No matter what the world tells you from this day forward, your definition of success is in that toast. You don't need to worry about other people's opinions about what you want to do or want to be in life anymore. If you ever needed permission to define success on your own terms, we're giving it to you now. This is what you should give your attention and energy to. If you notice, "Huh, I do not want to be remembered for having a really successful career," then you no longer need to pursue your next big job with so much intensity. Instead, pursue what you wrote down. If you measured success as your "Level of Joy & Fulfillment" instead of using dollar signs, how would you adjust your lifestyle?

How you define success is not up for debate. Let the world have their opinions. You are the only one who owns your life and controls where it will lead.

Your vision of success should become your beacon. Let it be the thing that gets you out of bed every day. If your WHY doesn't make you emotional, it may not be the right one. *Finding Your WHY* involves knowing what your life would feel meaningless without — exploring, laughing, learning, serving, and connecting are just some of the WHYs people have identified in our coaching conversations.

Nearly every decision you make in life will require trade-offs. You might get a little more of this (freedom), and a little less of this (money), so it's a constant reconciliation between what you're giving up and what you're gaining. What you need to know is how to make these trade-offs with integrity because you know yourself. This inner integrity allows you to confidently say "HECK YES!" or provide a thoughtful "NO" to the choices that come your way.

EXERCISE 7:
My Success Statement 2.0

Compare your 80th Birthday Speech to how you defined success in Exercise 5 ("My Definition of Success"). Are these descriptions aligned? If they are different, what stands out to you? Where did your definition of success come from?

Capture what you notice about the similarities and differences and revise your Personal Success Statement as needed in the space below:

Is this what Z looks like for you? If not, what's missing?

EXERCISE 8:
Realizing My Values

Values are important to understand because they help us make more confident choices and appreciate why others make different choices than we would. Your values drive your behavior, whether you are aware of them or not. Therefore, creating awareness of your values can turn confusion into clarity on your path to Z.

On the following pages, there is a list of words that are potential **Values** for you to consider. Even larger than the list we've provided are all the words in the world – and some of those might be more applicable to you. Feel free to capture what you value most in life in your own words. This list is just to help get your brain moving. In this exercise, we will be asking you to circle the **Values** that are the most important to you. Before you begin, here are some tips for identifying your **Values**.

TIPS FOR SELECTING YOUR VALUES

 Keep It Real

If you circle what you think *should be* important to you instead of the values you actually use when making life decisions, you did it wrong. The best way to do this exercise is to consider a very real choice that you have made within the last year or two:

- Did you start a new job?
- Did you need to make a significant financial investment?
- Did you have to say *no* to something that you were tempted to say *yes* to?

Think about those real choices and what your priorities were at the time. What are the real "filters" you used to decide what was the right or wrong choice for you? What were you most afraid of losing or gaining when you made that choice?

Certainly, your values adjust over time as you grow up and circumstances change, but in this moment: What is real and consistently true about how you make choices in life. Don't choose values you desire if you don't really see them showing up in your life in a real way. If you really had *those* values, you should see evidence of those values driving your behavior in life. You might really WANT the value of say, *Simplicity*, but if you have an overbooked schedule and a cluttered home, do you REALLY value *Simplicity*? You may aspire to it, but it's really not driving your actual behavior today — so don't choose it.

 ## *It's Okay to Admit It*

Sometimes values can feel like ugly truths. You know what really motivates you and you crave it. You might worry it seems unattractive to admit it (e.g., *Wealth, Admiration, Control*) but if you don't circle those words, then you are failing to recognize how much they matter to you and shape you. Circle what's real.

 ## **Go Deeper**

Maybe you work hard and don't want to relocate your family because you value things like *Stability* and *Safety*. Maybe you are faithful to your partner because you value things like *Honesty* and *Integrity*. The best words are the ones that go below the surface into the heart of motivation. Look deeper inside yourself for the real sources of truth in this exercise.

STEP 1: SELECT YOUR TOP VALUES

With the previous tips in mind, review the list that follows. **Read every single word** listed and notice your reactions to them. Circle the words that feel important to you — these are the things you long for more of and hold most dear when making life decisions. We also want you to Cross Out any words that feel unimportant to you. These are things you DO NOT value or take into consideration when evaluating choices in your life.

Acceptance	Communication	Empowerment
Accomplishment	Community	Encouragement
Accountability	Compassion	Endurance
Accuracy	Competence	Energy
Achievement	Competition	Enjoyment
Acknowledgment	Completion	Entertaining
Action	Concentration	Enthusiasm
Adventure	Confidence	Equality
Affection	Connection	Ethical
Altruism	Consistency	Excellence
Ambition	Contentment	Excitement
Amusement	Control	Exhilaration
Assertiveness	Cooperation	Experiences
Attentiveness	Coordinating	Expertise
Attractiveness	Courage	Exploration
Autonomy	Courtesy	Fairness
Awareness	Creativity	Faith
Balance	Credibility	Family
Beauty	Curiosity	Fame
Boldness	Decisiveness	Fearlessness
Bravery	Dedication	Feelings
Brilliance	Democracy	Fidelity
Calm	Dependability	Financial Freedom
Candor	Determination	Focus
Career	Devotion	Foresight
Certainty	Dignity	Fortitude
Challenge	Discipline	Freedom
Charity	Discovery	Friendship
Clarity	Diversity	Fun
Cleanliness	Drive	Frugality
Cleverness	Education	Generosity
Collaboration	Effectiveness	Genius
Comfort	Efficiency	Gentleness
Commitment	Elegance	Giving
Common Sense	Empathy	Goodness

Grace	Liberty	Potential
Gratitude	Logic	Power
Greatness	Love	Practical
Growth	Loyalty	Presence
Happiness	Magic	Preparation
Hard Work	Magnificence	Preservation
Harmony	Mastery	Privacy
Health	Maturity	Productivity
Helping Others	Meaning	Progress
Honesty	Ministering to Others	Professionalism
Honor	Moderation	Prosperity
Hope	Money	Protection
Humility	Motivation	Purpose
Humor	Music	Quality
Imagination	Nature	Realism
Improvement	Nutrition	Reasonable
Independence	Obedience	Recognition
Individuality	Openness	Recreation
Influence	Optimism	Reflection
Innovation	Organization	Relationships
Inspiration	Originality	Religion
Integrity	Parenting	Resourcefulness
Intellect	Passion	Respect
Intensity	Patience	Responsibility
Intimacy	Peace	Restraint
Intuition	Perfection	Results
Involvement	Performance	Reverence
Irreverence	Perseverance	Risk-Taking
Joy	Persistence	Romance
Justice	Personal Growth	Satisfaction
Kindness	Physical Challenge	Security
Knowledge	Planning	Self-Control
Laughter	Playfulness	Self-Expression
Leadership	Pleasure	Self-Reliance
Learning	Poise	Selflessness

Sensitivity	Sustainability	Uplifting
Sensuality	Talent	Valor
Serenity	Taste	Victory
Service	Teaching	Vigor
Sharing	Teamwork	Visionary
Significance	Temperance	Vitality
Silence	Tenderness	Vulnerability
Simplicity	Thankfulness	Wealth
Sincerity	Thorough	Welcoming
Skillfulness	Thoughtful	Winning
Smart	Timeliness	Wisdom
Social Change	Thrilling	Wit
Solitude	Tolerance	Work
Spirituality	Toughness	
Spontaneity	Traditional	*ADD YOUR VALUES IF*
Sportsmanship	Tranquility	*THEY ARE NOT LISTED:*
Stability	Transparency	
Status	Travel	_____
Stewardship	Trust	
Strength	Trustworthy	_____
Structure	Truth	
Success	Understanding	_____
Supportive	Uniqueness	
Surprise	United	_____

STEP 2: YOUR TOP 5 VALUES

Okay, now it's time to get REALLY REAL. How many did you circle – more than 20? Well, we need to narrow that list down and get clearer on what you value most – really zero in on the key things that matter. **Take the number of items you circled and narrow it down to only your Top 5 values**. Yes, only 5. It doesn't mean that the others don't matter, but they don't matter as much as those five do. You can do it! If you really struggle to get the list down to 5, start by narrowing down to your Top 10. Then, really examine those 10 until you can pare down to the Top 5 – don't short cut this step!

If you are struggling to choose between words, get out of your head and check your gut.

Write your Top 5 Values below:

1. _____
2. _____
3. _____
4. _____
5. _____

Step back and look at that list. Are these words actually the CRITERIA you use to guide your life decisions? Does seeing them all listed together synthesize or crystallize something for you? In looking at your Top 5 Values, are they aligned with the trade-offs and choices you are making in your life right now? Are any of these values holding you back? Do you want to change any of them? Refine your list until you feel clear about your Top 5 Values at this point in your life.

STEP 3: RANKING YOUR VALUES

Speaking of trade-offs, for the final step in this exercise, you will rank your Top 5 Values in order of priority. At the top of the list (#1) should be the value that, if it really came down to it, would be your single guiding light in life. The best approach for this prioritization exercise is to imagine that JOB #1 offered you an abundance of one of your Top 5 Values, and JOB #2 offered you an abundance of another. Make them exclusive choices. For example, JOB #1 will provide you more *Independence* and JOB #2 will give you more *Security*. Which one would you choose? Rank that Value higher.

MY TOP 5 VALUES IN ORDER OF IMPORTANCE

1. _____
2. _____
3. _____
4. _____
5. _____

Input these new coordinates into your GPS and check-in periodically to make sure that these values are influencing your life choices. If not, you are either acting out of alignment with what you say you value, or your values have shifted. Honoring your Values will bring you closer to your personal definition of Z.

GO FURTHER!

Reflect on your values with someone in your life. Share what you realized as you completed this exercise and ask them to explore the following questions with you. *NOTE: You might encourage them to do the Values exercise as well so you can talk about how your individual values impact your relationship.* Some additional questions to explore:

- What has shaped my values? Why are they my Top 5?

- To what extent have these always been my values? To what extent have they changed over time? What has caused them to shift or change?

- Describe how your current life choices are ALIGNED or NOT ALIGNED with your values right now.

- Are there any values "holding you back?" For example, some people value things that steer them toward unfulfilling work or "*Safe*" choices. Be curious about the potential "dark side" of your values.

Life has meaning only if you do what is meaningful to you. ❞

ALAN COHEN

CANDYCE AND MICHELLE'S VALUES

Your values will be different from everyone else's, including how you define those values and how they influence the decisions you make. We are including ours below as an example. Even if you have chosen the exact same words we have, the meaning you attach to them could be different. That is okay – that is exactly how you get clearer about your WHY. You can see below that we share two of the same values but define them differently.

Michelle's Values and What They Mean to Her

- FREEDOM – Ability to do what I want, when I want – free from burden
- FULFILLMENT – Spending time doing things that matter and make a difference
- GRATITUDE – Appreciation and recognition for all the good things in my life
- GRACE – Permission to make mistakes and forgive myself
- CONNECTION – Cultivating and nurturing key relationships

Candyce's Values and What They Mean to Her

- WOW – Creating and experiencing unforgettable moments
- CONNECTION – Deeper relationships, deeper conversations
- INSPIRATION – Work that is inspired by faith, and work that inspires others
- FREEDOM – Financially, professionally, geographically
- IMPACT – Leaving a lasting impression wherever I go

EXERCISE 9:
My Bold Goals

Now that you have defined your Personal Definition of Success, and identified your Top 5 Values, let's get specific about what you really want in life. In this section, you will create two "Bold Goals" — these are ambitious undertakings, things you would be willing to work hard at achieving as you sense they would leap-frog you forward in the alphabet. We encourage you to think of Bold Goals for both your personal and professional lives. If you don't work outside the home, your goal for your professional life could be volunteer work or related to the role you play in your family. **These goals should be aligned with your values and make you feel more successful.**

Bold Goals help you grow as a person in a way that matters to you. Reaching these goals would help you make significant progress toward your Z. What have you always wanted to learn or experience? What's something you have not accomplished yet? For your professional goal it may be leading a team, developing a new product, starting your own business, or being able to work from anywhere in the world. As we said before, your professional goal doesn't have to be related to making more money or moving up the corporate ladder. For example, if you are a stay-at-home parent — What is a goal you could set that would add meaning to your role as a stay-at-home parent? A friend of ours wanted to teach her kids how to do their own laundry, once she did, it freed up hours of her time each week. She spent that time reading books she'd wanted to read for years! It felt like progress, big progress, which made it a great goal!

For your personal goal, listen to your heart. If you think of something that makes you say, "Oh, that would be amazing, but it's impossible," don't dismiss it. It might just be the perfect one! Does it make you nervous or cause a tingly feeling in the pit of your stomach to imagine it being your reality? If so, write it down. Check-in with your body and don't censor yourself. Maybe it is restoring a fixer-upper in the country, or becoming a yoga instructor, or traveling to Fiji and staying in a bungalow on the water. If you *really* want it, write it down.

If you are still thinking, "I don't know what to write!" That's okay. Write down what you do know. Make it vivid, specific, and exciting! Have you heard of *SMART* goals? Well, normally SMART stands for *Specific, Measureable, Actionable, Realistic,* and *Timely*. For the purpose of this exercise; however, SMART stands for *Specific, Monumental, Actionable, Resonating,* and *Thrilling*! Go ahead and DREAM!

MY BOLD PROFESSIONAL GOAL:

WHY DO I WANT THIS? (What is your motivation to do this? Check your values!)

MY BOLD PERSONAL GOAL:

WHY DO I WANT THIS? (What is your motivation to do this? Check your values!)

GO FURTHER!

How did it feel to write down your Bold Goals? Check-in with yourself and notice how you feel when you imagine reaching those goals. Do you feel excited and energized? Or do you already feel overwhelmed and proactively skeptical? Sometimes fear and overwhelm causes us to not even try to accomplish the things we say we want. We can limit ourselves by selecting only "reasonable" or "realistic" goals because we don't want to fail. Maybe your inner critic (who we call your *Backseat Driver* – more on them later in the book!) whispers scolding words of shame and reminds you that dreaming of Fiji is irresponsible because you should spend money on more practical things – like home repair projects and college tuition. But if your screensaver features a bungalow over crystal clear water and you spend hours daydreaming about reading in that hammock and the feel of the ocean breeze on your face…then you know traveling to Fiji would make you very, very happy. Fiji would be a WOW! Fiji would be a great time to connect with your husband! Fiji is worth it! Make this a Personal Goal for yourself and start saving!

The reason we are encouraging you to create and pursue these Bold Goals in your life is that they connect you to your inner sources of motivation. When your goals are aligned to your values you are going to have the stamina to chase them.

Setting a Bold Goal is only the first step. The next step is to share it with others. Did you know that "Secret Goals" are far less likely to be reached? For some people, sharing their dreams is the scariest part. They tell themselves stories about how others will react or judge them. One of our coaching clients flat out said, "I can't tell my family about this because they will freak out. They would start to worry about how it impacts them and try to stop me." How many times have you pulled the brakes on your dreams when you thought about how others in your life would react? The question we asked them was, "Is it possible they might NOT react that way if they knew how much it meant to you?" Once he acknowledged the possibility, we encouraged him to share his current letter in the alphabet, and which letter he would reach if he made the change he wanted to make. To his delight, his family acknowledged how unhappy he had been at work and encouraged him to take a step back. They also celebrated when he landed his new (lower-level) role and achieved the work-life balance he so desperately desired.

So go tell it on the mountain! Share your goals and enroll others in helping you reaching them!

Safe is good for sidewalks and swimming pools, but life requires risk if we are to get anywhere.

SIMON SINEK

GAUGE CHECK: HOW CLEAR ARE YOU FEELING ABOUT YOUR WHY?

We hope the exercises and stories in this section have helped you gain more clarity about your WHY. The words you have circled and written on these pages reveal insights that are core to you discovering your purpose and living a more a fulfilling life. You should feel empowered to define success for yourself and motivated to reach the Bold Goals you set in this chapter. You have answered some truly life-changing questions…questions that some people wait their whole lives to explore! You are well on your way to *Finding Your Z!*

Draw a line that indicates your current level of clarity after reading *Finding Your WHY.*

I know why I make the decisions I do. I can clearly and confidently articulate what matters most to me – including my values, my goals, and my personal definition of success.

UNCLEAR **CLEAR**

REFLECTING ON FINDING YOUR WHY

Questions We Explored

- What is the impact I want to make in the world?

- What matters most to me? What are my values?

- What is my personal definition of success?

- What are the goals I want to set for myself to have a more meaningful life?

Now, let's go find your WHO.

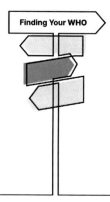

Finding Your WHO

Chapter 4:

FINDING YOUR WHO

FINDING YOUR WHO
Questions to Explore

- When you imagine your ideal life, who are the people you want beside you?

- Who are the most influential people in your life?

- What impact do these people have on your life decisions – both positively and negatively?

The people in our lives can be sources of inspiration or sabotage as we work to accomplish our goals. Understanding the level of influence we allow people to have on our life decisions is important if we want to be successful and have meaningful relationships. We don't do life alone. We intentionally choose the relationships we invest in and we can either help or hinder those people from realizing their Z too.

Mario's Story

Mario is an example of someone who has prioritized the WHO factors in nearly every life decision he has made. Mario grew up in a small town, married his high school sweetheart, and bought a house down the road from his parents and siblings. To this day, his high school friends continue to be his closest friends. He went to college within 20 minutes of where he grew up and accepted a job at a local manufacturing company. Mario has been very successful professionally, climbing to the highest levels of the company he has helped build and lead for the past 25 years. Despite many job offers that could have taken him onto bigger companies with larger salaries, he chose to stay where he was. From an outsider's perspective, you might think he played it safe – that he chose to stay in his comfort zone by living in his hometown with his high school sweetheart, but that was not the case at all.

Throughout his career and personal life, he deliberately planted and cultivated his roots in the hometown where he was born. As a result, his children have had the opportunity to build close relationships with their grandparents, aunts, uncles, and cousins. They have been blessed with built-in babysitters and dog sitters just down the road. When his father became ill with cancer and later passed away, he was there. He was able to attend every oncologist appointment, help his parents navigate the complex world of health insurance and Medicare, and ensure that when his dad passed nothing was left unsaid. He held his mother's hand while his father slipped away and grieved alongside his siblings. Now, he is grateful that he lives close to his mother and can help her live life without her husband anytime she needs him.

This was a life he chose on purpose. He wanted his parents nearby to cheer on their grandkids at basketball games, to fix his mom's leaky faucet, and to enjoy Sunday dinners with his siblings arguing about which team would win the football game. Mario prioritized WHO over all other factors and has never regretted it for a single moment.

FINDING YOUR WHO

Reflecting on WHO is important in context with WHY, WHAT, and WHERE, as we don't often make decisions in isolation. We make decisions about WHO we want to live close to, spend time with, provide for, or make proud. We often run our choices past these people and value their feedback.

Inevitably, the choices you make on your path to Z will impact your WHO. All the people in your life are on their own paths, so it is reasonable for them to have opinions about how your Z intersects with theirs. Using the *Finding Your Z* framework can be an effective tool for conversations with these people regarding decisions you are considering. It allows them to understand your perspective as well as share their own. If you are offered a job that helps you reach a new income level, but it involves spending less time at home, it will certainly affect those that live with you and love you. These decisions require talking about the trade-offs you are or aren't willing to make on your path to Z. The simplicity of the framework will hopefully provide a common language that helps you evaluate those trade-offs together.

Many people will not realize their Z unless certain individuals are there to enjoy it with them. Like Mario, you might correlate the quality of your life with the quality of your connections to others. How many life decisions, including career decisions, have you made based upon WHO factors?

WHO Factors include:

- **WHO You Want to Live Closer To (or farther away from)**
- **Your Marital Status**
- **Your Children (Do you want children? How many?)**
- **Family Members**
- **Friends**

- **Community / Church**
- **Co-Workers**
- **Leaders**
- **Neighbors**
- **Mentors or Mentees**

Have you ever made a career decision based upon a WHO factor? Chosen roles because you wanted to spend more time with certain people or move on from others? Have you made tradeoffs to save money and pay for what they needed or the dreams you wanted to realize together? Most people consider their WHO when making career decisions, but it is rarely mentioned in any career management book. This is one of the main reasons the *Finding Your Z* model was developed to share with people – people need a more wholehearted and inclusive way to weigh ALL the factors that need to be considered when building an ideal life.

The concepts in *Finding Your Z* include the conversations companies don't hire us to have with their employees – but we believe that these are the questions and conversations people *should* have with their teammates when helping them manage their careers. We have personally facilitated six different "Career Development Workshops" for six different companies. These programs are always called something like "Managing Your Career at ABC Company," or "Building Your Brand at XYZ Company." You can imagine what goes on in those workshops, right? These classes are designed to tell people how to get ahead in Corporate America, and specifically within their current company. That is a really narrow way to think about career decisions. People don't, or shouldn't, make life decisions in a vacuum and ignore the other facets of their life that will be significantly impacted. The quality of your relationships, or the WHO factor, is a significant contributor to a person's wellbeing and happiness. We want to challenge people to think beyond their career when they seek fulfillment because it isn't found solely in salary bands and titles.

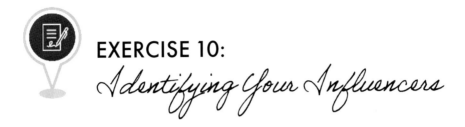

EXERCISE 10:
Identifying Your Influencers

n this exercise, we will ask you to **identify the 10 most influential people in your life**. This includes your family, friends, neighbors, colleagues, managers, and mentors. Not unlike your values, there may be some "ugly truths" when you think about your influencers. You may realize there are people who influence your life choices, that shouldn't. If their influence impacts your thinking or what you decide to do on a regular basis, put them on the list. If you run your life choices by Kate Busybody at the bus stop, and you think about what she'd say before you make a decision, then she's an influencer – put her on the list. Even if you are thinking, "But I don't even like Kate," you still need write her down! Kate shapes your thinking until you make the choice to remove her influence.

Consider these questions:

- When something big happens in my life, who do I want to tell first?
- Who do I turn to when I am struggling to make a decision?
- Who are the people I seek approval from?
- Whose opinions matter most to me?

THE 10 MOST INFLUENTIAL PEOPLE IN MY LIFE

1. _____

2. _____

3. _____

4. _____

5. _____

6. _____

7. _____

8. _____

9. _____

10. _____

GO FURTHER!

- Are there people you listed who you wish were **NOT** on your list? Or people **NOT** listed here that surprise you?
- When you think about the quality of your relationships with those on this list, are they where you want them to be? If not, why?
- Would any of these individuals be surprised to see themselves on your list? Are you on theirs?
- Does the level of time and energy you invest in these relationships align with how much they influence you?

Look at the list and assess where each of these relationships currently stand in terms of:

- ✓ *Frequency*: How much time do you spend together?

- ✓ *Proximity*: To what extent is physical distance impacting their influence in your life?

- ✓ *Depth*: To what extent do these people truly know you? How vulnerable and honest are you with them?

- ✓ *Power*: If you could weigh the magnitude of their influence in your life, whose voices carry the most weight?

For some people, the 10 Most Influential People in their lives are helping them get ahead. But for others, the people who influence them are lovingly sabotaging their happiness and progress. We will help you thoughtfully determine who is influencing your life now, and who you want to influence your life in the future. To do this, we use the metaphor of YOU being the star of a traveling rock band. We will stretch the road trip metaphor a little bit on this one, but stick with us!

Imagine you get off the tour bus and step out onto the stage – it's just you, standing there under the lights. The arena is packed with all the people in your life. They are all interested in what you are doing, but to varying degrees. Some are on-stage jamming alongside you, some are cheering at the top of their lungs, and some are just scrolling on their phones giving you an occasional head nod. And some of them are actively hoping you will trip and fall on your face.

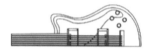

Who Are Your Bandmates?

At the heart of your life is your Band. Your Bandmates are your biggest supporters. They want to help you become the person you're capable of being. They actively offer their time and energy to help you reach your goals. They tell you the truth and provide feedback to help you, not tear you down. They know your story and champion your success. They make you better and challenge you to think bigger. Oftentimes, they have experienced their own success and failures and can offer helpful advice, but they also recognize that you are a unique individual on your own path. They help remove barriers, introduce you to their networks, and come to the party when it is time to celebrate your success. They will be there to remind you of how strong and capable you are, even when you forget it yourself. They ACCELERATE your ambitions. These are the people you want closest to you, in your ear, when you step onto the biggest, scariest stages.

Who Are Your Fans?

These are the people in your life who support you and think you're great, but they rarely offer their time or energy to help you reach your goals. You care what they think, though! If they criticize you or stop cheering for you, it might hurt your feelings.

Your interactions with them may feel like a cheery high-five. When you tell them about something you are working on or want to do in your life, they might say, "That's awesome! Good luck with that! You rock," but then they largely wait around to buy the book, or come to your housewarming party, or *like* your Instagram pictures. They don't actively tear you down or stop your progress, but they don't accelerate it either. You may value their support, but they have a NEUTRAL impact when it comes to making the music happen.

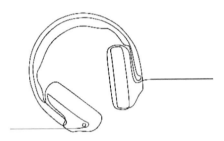

Who Do You Keep in the Cheap Seats?

These are the individuals in your life who distract you from your ambitions. They intentionally or lovingly sabotage you with their own fear and negativity. They might have the best of intentions, but they are often more concerned about how your decisions will affect them, which becomes their focus. They may disguise their opinions as an expression of concern for you — "I just don't want you to be hurt or disappointed." They might mention the things that could go wrong and fail to see the possibilities — "But what if you hate it and waste all of your money for nothing?" Your interactions with them may feel like letting the air out of your Dream Balloon or POPPING it entirely. They likely haven't taken risks in their own lives, or have had bad experiences, or fear that you will make a mistake and resent them for not speaking up. It is important to recognize that they are throwing your dreams in REVERSE and holding you back. These are the voices you need to manage most — we suggest keeping them in the metaphorical "cheap seats" to ensure you can stay focused and don't become weighed down by their negative commentaries.

EXERCISE 11:
Creating Your Seating Chart

Use the Seating Chart image below to place the names of people who are sitting in each section of your life today. Who are Your Bandmates? Who are your Fans? Who do you currently keep in the Cheap Seats?

Plot THE 10 MOST INFLUENTIAL PEOPLE IN YOUR LIFE in the image below.

Who do you keep in the cheap seats?

Who are your fans?

Who is in your band?

THE CHEAP SEATS:
These people may be intentionally, or lovingly sabotaging you with their fear and negativity. They distract you from your ambitions. They throw your dreams in **REVERSE**.

YOUR FANS:
These people support you and congratulate you, but they don't help you make the music. You care about their opinion, and it would hurt if they criticized you, because you seek their approval. They influence your path to Z, but they are parked in **NEUTRAL** when it comes to actually helping you achieve your goals.

YOUR BAND:
The individuals in Your Band not only encourage you but they help you become who you want to be. They actively support you and offer their help as you work to reach your goals. They make you better. They remind you of how great you are and **ACCELERATE** your ambitions. You can't imagine getting to Z without them.

GO FURTHER!

As you look your seating chart, WHO stands out?

What surprises you when looking at the seat assignments for the "10 Most Influential People in Your Life?

Are people seated where they NEED TO BE to realize your ideal life? If not, what needs to change?

“Show me your friends and I will show you your future.**”**

MOOSA RAHAT

LET'S TALK ABOUT THOSE PEOPLE IN THE CHEAP SEATS

Putting someone you love in the Cheap Seats can feel wrong and hurtful. You don't stop loving someone just because you seat them in a place that allows you to feel healthy and confident on-stage. It also doesn't mean you have a bad relationship with them. You might just be setting boundaries – consciously selecting what you share and mindfully involving them in your life. People you love can and do sabotage you – and they often aren't aware they are doing it. It can be packaged as love, but it doesn't serve you and your goals. We always tell people, "If you set a healthy boundary in your relationship, and they get angry with you for it, then they are currently benefiting from you not having it."

For example, one of our colleagues recently moved to New York when she was selected to be the editor of a major newspaper out east – this was the job she worked her whole life to land! Moving to New York meant she would no longer see her parents on a weekly basis. Her mother said she was proud of her, but then started weeping and listing all of the holidays they'd miss together. She talked about all the sleepless nights she would spend worrying about her daughter when she moved to the Big City. She talked about how old they were getting and how much they would miss having her nearby. It was a HEARTSTRING-PLUCKING MASTERCLASS.

The people we love the most are the one most impacted by our decisions – displaying strong emotions is a normal reaction to change. People may feel fearful, angry, or sad when we do something they wouldn't choose for us to do. So your mom/best friend/boss will use whatever emotional power, influence, and pressure they can muster to change your mind.

This type of behavior doesn't make someone a bad person. You can just see it for what it is, and not overinvest your time trying to get them to be excited about your big plans or your new job. Our colleague chose to remind her mom of how she left her home country of Puerto Rico to pursue a better life in the United States and chase her dreams. She also used the framework of the alphabet to show her mom how many letters forward this move would take her toward her ideal life. It helped, somewhat – but her mom still cries. By that way - she loves her new job, and has no regrets!

OTHER PEOPLE'S OPINIONS

Another group of people you want to keep in the Cheap Seats are not close to you at all, but their voices can absolutely influence you. Isn't it interesting how sometimes you care more about what your neighbor or a person on social media thinks than someone who really matters in your life? It is something to pay attention to, because it can subtly change how you think about your goals and your sense of progress.

In her book *Daring Greatly*, Brené Brown talks about a quote from Teddy Roosevelt that she keeps in her office. This quote is one we have now framed and refer to because dream chasing is humbling work.

> **"It is not the critic who counts. Not the man who points out how the strong man stumbles or where the doer of deeds could have done better. The credit belongs to the man who is actually in the arena, whose face is marred by dust and sweat and blood, who strives valiantly, who errs and comes up short again and again and again – because there is no effort without error or shortcoming. But he who knows the great enthusiasms, the great devotions, who spends himself for a worthy cause; Who, at the best, knows, in the end, the triumph of high achievement, and who, if he fails, at least he fails while daring greatly, so that his place shall never be with those cold and timid souls who knew neither victory or defeat."**
>
> **~ Teddy Roosevelt**

She goes on to say, "If you're not in the arena, also getting your ass kicked, I'm not interested in your feedback." *Whoa.* That line made us sit back in our chairs as we are not immune from the challenges of *Finding Your Z*. In fact, we didn't touch this book for OVER A YEAR because we were barely hanging on in our daily lives as bosses and moms. While the majority of people in our lives were fans of this book idea, and encouraged us in every way imaginable, one individual suggested that, "It was a lot of time to spend on something that may or may not sell" (as if we weren't already afraid of that). We had to decide who we wanted to listen to – this skeptic or the people we've coached that can't wait to share this book with their families, kids, and teammates? Wasn't the promise of helping countless people change their lives worth more than this one person's doubts?

Listening to OPO – *Other People's Opinions* – can be a real motivation killer. Sometimes these "Other People" are ones you don't even know! You might be a real independent thinker, but the rest of us like to research things on the internet, read books, and listen to podcasts. This information can change our opinion about what is the right or wrong thing to do. How many times have you heard someone use the phrase, "They say that …" in that past year? As in, "They say that 90% of businesses fail within their first year." Who is "they" anyway? And why do we immediately imagine ourselves in the 90% instead of the 10% when we hear stuff like that?

Tell us if you can relate – You share some exciting news on social media ("I'm writing a book! I'm getting certified in massage therapy! I'm starting a woodworking business!") and you immediately think about what your high school nemesis would say and imagine them cheering for you to fail. Why do we care about them and what they think? We didn't like them in high school so why are we allowing them to impact our decisions as a grown-ass adult? (By the way, guilty as charged! We totally felt that when we started promoting this book.) It is easy to buy into the cultural narratives suggesting that you may not have the right education, the right title, or the right background to accomplish what you say you want to do. Society's expectations of you may not be aligned with your own ambitions. So turn the "THEM" dial down, and turn the "YOU" volume up. Put on some Kelly Clarkson and remind yourself that, "You know you've got this, because you have had it all along."

You are the one in the arena. Your face is the one marred with dust and blood. Don't give those people any more of your mindshare because they haven't done what you are about to do.

LIFE AS A ONE-MAN BAND

When we created the "Seating Chart" exercise we were keenly aware that this could be a real gut-punch moment for some people. We know countless individuals who have been continuously let down and disappointed by the people in their lives. Or maybe they have lost some of their Bandmates and Fans, which has left them feeling very alone and insecure up on that stage. If this is you, we hope you prioritize finding some new members for your Band and start building back your Fan base. You are still the same Star you have always been and the world still needs to hear your music. Please don't stop touring! We are cheering for you!

It can feel impossible, or at least daunting, to build new relationships that are worthy of becoming a Bandmate. We recommend becoming really clear about the qualities you are looking for before signing any contracts.

- **Front Door Check:** Seek out people who consistently lift you up and make you feel better when you're around them. When they walk out your front door, you should find yourself smiling, thinking about how much you love being around them, and how much you love who *you are* when they are around.

- **Be Specific:** It might be helpful to label the unique qualities needed in Your Bandmates and deliberately seek out those qualities in future relationships.

- **Level Up:** Find people who are further along on their path to Z so they will motivate you to reach yours!

Research suggests that we are deeply impacted by the five people closest to us in our lives. WHO you spend time with and listen to can be a game changer! People who are more successful than you are not jealous of your accomplishments and will encourage you to keep going.

Armed with this new knowledge, take a look at the names you put in each section of Your Seating Chart. Are these people where they need to be?

Use this fresh Seating Chart to move people where they **NEED TO BE** to reach your dreams. You can also identify new people you want to add, even if you but don't know them yet (mentors, new relationships, etc.).

YOUR IDEAL SEATING CHART

Who do you keep in the cheap seats?

Who are your fans?

Who is in your band?

66 The cynics may be the loudest voices – but I promise you, they will accomplish the least. **99**

BARACK OBAMA

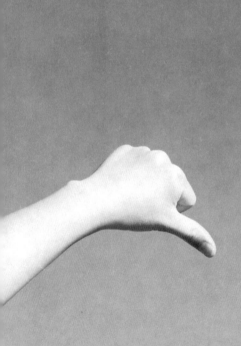

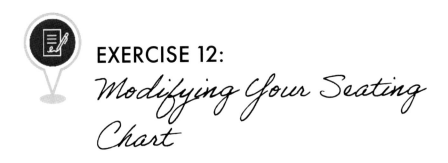

EXERCISE 12:
Modifying Your Seating Chart

Finding *Your WHO* invites you to consider how other people are impacting your life choices. Some difficult feelings may have surfaced during that last exercise, or maybe it generated some *Ah-Ha* moments. You may have some work to do to get your relationships where they need to be.

Maybe You...

- Realized people are lovingly sabotaging you
- Have fallen out of touch with a friend that matters to you
- Are longing for a significant other in your life
- Need a mentor or a confidante
- Need to expand your professional network
- Need to rebuild a broken relationship from your past
- Want to have a hard conversation with someone

What are the actions you want to take after reading this chapter?

How will those actions get you closer to living your ideal life (your Z)?

Through these exercises and your personal reflections, we hope you feel clearer and more confident about the impact and influence that WHO has on your life. By identifying the people in Your Band, the people who are Your Fans, and those individuals who need to be in the Cheap Seats, you should realize that you are not alone on this journey. There are people who will support and lift you up as you do the work of *Finding Your Z*.

GAUGE CHECK: HOW CLEAR ARE YOU FEELING ABOUT YOUR WHO NOW?

We hope the exercises and stories in this section have helped you gain more clarity about your WHO. These insights that will help you build more intentional relationships, and not forget WHO matters most when making big life decisions.

Draw a line that indicates your current level of clarity after reading *Finding Your WHO*.

I know WHO the most important people are in my life and will intentionally include them in my journey. I know how to manage the influence they have on my decisions.

UNCLEAR   **CLEAR**

REFLECTING ON FINDING YOUR WHO

Questions We Explored

- When you imagine your ideal life, who are the people you want beside you?

- Who are the most influential people in your life?

- What impact do these people have on your life decisions — both positively and negatively?

Now, let's go find your WHERE!

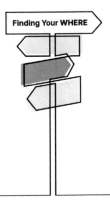

Finding Your WHERE

Chapter 5:

FINDING
YOUR WHERE

FINDING YOUR WHERE

Questions to Explore

- Where is my happy place?

- What is my ideal lifestyle?

- What am I doing when I feel most myself or most alive?

Research suggests that WHERE you live may be the single greatest contributor to your happiness and well-being. *Finding Your WHERE* encourages you to describe the environment where you can enjoy your best life.

Michelle's Story

I grew up around lakes my entire life — my grandparents, and now parents, have a lake cabin that I spent time visiting every summer. It was a part of my childhood memories and a place where the entire family would gather together to enjoy the short and sweet summer months in Minnesota.

But, it was more than that. I found myself drawn to the water for its ability to provide me the peace, calm, and clarity that I longed for in my life. Growing up, anytime something was going on that I needed to sort out, I didn't look any further than the end of my grandparents' dock. There I would dangle my feet in the water and look out over the lake in silence. It would immediately put my mind into a state where I could deal with anything. I need the water the way some people need oxygen — it is a part of me and made me who I am.

As a result, I prioritized living by the water in my adult life. For years, I enjoyed summers at my grandparents' cabin, but that just wasn't enough. As I got older, I began scouring newspapers and websites for a lakeshore property of my own. I told everyone that I was going to live on a lake someday. I attended Open Houses of homes for sale on lakes, even when the financial reality of buying one was several years away. Then one day the stars aligned, and I found the perfect house on a lake about 20 minutes from my job and my husband's job. We now have the lake home we always dreamed of and can experience the peace and focus of being by the water every day (except for the months of December through March, where it is primarily ice). The point is that I made it a priority, believed it was possible, and kept going until I made it happen. This is what it means to find your WHERE. It is where you feel complete — where you become your best self.

FINDING YOUR WHERE

One of our favorite conversation starters at a dinner party is asking people to describe their *Happy Place*. It is fascinating how different people interpret that question — sometimes they describe a specific destination like Hawaii or their cabin. Others focus more on a type of activity or experience they enjoy — like riding their mountain bike, floating on an air mattress in a swimming pool, or baking bread in their kitchen. Regardless, there are always important Z insights to pay attention to in their response. We will ask you to answer it in just a few minutes.

To get your inspired response, let's consider all the different variables that have already influenced WHERE you enjoy spending time. If you are at a point of transition in your life — graduating, retiring, or getting a divorce — these questions might be well-timed!

HERE ARE SOME FACTORS TO CONSIDER:

 Climate: Do you prefer warm weather where you can live in flip-flops and shorts every day? Or do you love the fresh smell of snow and the whoosh of ice skates on a rink? Or do you just need to experience the change of seasons and want more moderate temps?

 Community: Are you searching for an idyllic Stars Hallow/Hallmark movie small town lifestyle? Or craving the buzz of a bigger city with more diverse cultures and cuisine? Do you want to be best friends with your neighbor, or live freely in the middle of nowhere?

Home Environment: What style of home do you dream of? Is it expansive with all of the upgrades, technology, and amenities available? Or a small, cozy place with minimal upkeep? Do you dream of white walls, clean lines, and minimal clutter or a home brimming with toys, picture frames, and wet swimsuits on the floor?

 External Environment: Do oceans, mountains, or farmland calm your spirit? Maybe it is in the woods, or in the desert, or on a boat? What do you enjoy looking out your window and seeing? What is the scenery you want in the background of your life?

 Activities: Is your passion yoga, skiing, shopping, or hiking? If you had an entire day to do whatever you wanted, what would you do?

 Daily Rituals: Is there a time of day that you treasure? A special place you like to go to unwind or connect with others?

 Proximity to Family and Friends: How important is it for you to have the people you love with you in your Happy Place?

 Lifestyle/Conveniences (Access to Goods & Services): What are the amenities that matter most to you? Restaurants, theaters, night life, arts, or other entertainment? How long of a commute do you want to work? What is the traffic like where you live?

 Availability of Jobs for Your Career/Industry: Are you able to earn a living in your Happy Place and afford the type of home you want to live in?

 Quality and Availability of Education and Healthcare: How important are the standards of education and healthcare at this point in your life?

 Safety: Will you and the people you love feel safe and secure there?

In reading those questions, you know which of the WHERE factors matter most to you, and you have probably already made life decisions that align with the lifestyle you desire. These factors impact your quality of life, and the higher your quality of life, the happier you will be. The happier you are, the more successful you will feel.

In his book, *The Blue Zones of Happiness*, Dan Buettner defines happiness as "life satisfaction" and he researched the places in the world where people tend to live the longest, happiest, healthiest lives. These places had a few things in common – a lot of sunshine, access to green spaces/nature, a readily available social network, shorter commutes to work, availability of meaningful work, a focus on fitness/health, and access to healthy food. His research suggests that where we live influences our happiness more than anything else!

We like calling it your Happy Place because certain places just give you a sense of comfort. They make you come alive and provide you with both energy and peace. These places recharge your batteries, help you breathe deeply, refocus, and reconnect with the best version of yourself. Close your eyes and think about where those places might be for you – what does it look like, feel like, sound like, and smell like when you are there?

To get clear about your WHERE, you need to check-in with your body.

- **WHERE do you feel most at home?**

- **WHERE do you wish you could stay, and never leave, because it feels so right when you are there?**

Read the following visualization and note any IMAGES or WORDS that feel important to you. The goal is to gain more clarity of your ideal lifestyle so you can further shape the vision of your WHERE as a part of your overall Z.

> *Imagine you are living your ideal life. You wake up in the morning in a place that feels like home. As you lie there, you look around and take it all in. Notice the details of where you are before you crawl out of bed. Notice how your home smells, sounds, looks, and feels. Who lives there with you?*

> *Now slowly walk over to the window and look outside. What are you looking at? What do you notice? Where is your home in the world and what do you appreciate about the view? Why did you choose to live here of all places?*

Now it is time to get ready for your day — you don't have any "must-do" responsibilities today, so you can do whatever you want. You intend to spend the day enjoying each of your favorite pastimes. What is the first thing you want to do? Who is with you? Notice how you feel imagining yourself enjoying this activity. Continue to play out your ideal day, one activity or moment at a time. Close your eyes and really notice what you would choose to spend your time doing.

Now imagine it is the end of your ideal day and you are sitting down that night to write in a journal. You begin to write down what you feel grateful for in your life. What are you writing? As you fall asleep you feel deeply peaceful and deeply fulfilled. You worked hard to have this life, but it was all worth it.

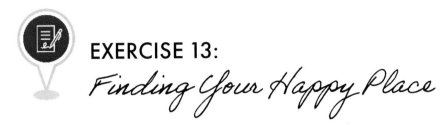

EXERCISE 13:
Finding Your Happy Place

Take a moment and reflect on what you just read. Once you have taken several minutes to visualize your ideal day, write down everything you thought of – what you saw, heard, smelled, felt. **Capture the words and images that came to your mind as you imagined your ideal life. Feel free to draw pictures or include inspirations for a future vision board in the space below.**

_____

_____

_____

_____

_____

_____

Beyond literal addresses and locations, where are your Happy Places?

_____

_____

_____

Does anything surprise you about your WHERE?

_____

_____

_____

To what extent have you found your WHERE already? What are some ideas you have for enjoying more of your WHERE places or experiences in life?

_____

_____

_____

How is your WHERE connected to your WHO, WHY, or WHAT?

_____

_____

_____

Double-click on some of the details in your vision. If you said you saw water outside your window, were you clear what type of water you were looking at (pool, ocean, river)? Did you fully capture the details of your home and neighborhood?

Try to go a little further in describing your Ideal Day.

_____

_____

_____

FINDING YOUR HAPPY PLACE

If your WHERE isn't someplace you already live, or can imagine yourself living (for whatever reason — financially or logistically), are there ways to have more of what you appreciate about it in your daily life? For example, Candyce's sister loves spending time at the family cabin where they have bonfires and make s'mores nearly every night. To bring herself joy in the off-season, she might choose to build a nice firepit at her house so she can roast marshmallows year-round.

When you realize that there is something that brings you joy, you need to prioritize spending more time doing that in your life. If you feel like you work all year for one week of vacation at the beach, you need to change that — 51 weeks of misery is not a life! Challenge your mindset and become creative on how you can add more of your WHERE to your days.

Your WHERE could be someone else's NO WAY. We run into this a lot; after all, we live in Minnesota. Minnesota is a wonderful place to live, for some people. But it is an extreme environment. If you live someplace where snow is on the ground for months at a time you better love all of the activities that go along with winter! If your family loves the S's — skating, sledding, skiing, snowshoeing, snowmobiling — and you long to see your kids outside playing hockey on the pond you built in your backyard, Minnesota really could be your Happy Place!

But if you are married to someone who feels a little bit of themselves disappear in the winter, then that is a problem. If they feel metaphorically pressed up against the glass asking if they will survive until spring, or they wear sweaters and shiver when it is 60 degrees outside, they will be counting the days until you move. These people dream of different S's – sitting on the beach, sipping margaritas, snorkeling, and sun-kissed cheeks. If that is the lifestyle they desire, Minnesota is not their happy place. Trust us.

Now you might be thinking, "But what if my whole family lives in Minnesota and wherever they are, is where I'm happiest. I can't imagine not being able to pop over to my sister's house for a cup of coffee or a glass of wine on a moment's notice." Then, maybe you choose to stay in Minnesota, and get a divorce. Just kidding. But you could agree to take a lot of vacations and allow your spouse to enjoy time in tropical climates each winter.

Your ideal WHERE will shift and change over time, during different seasons of your life. When people are young they may value the ability to walk to restaurants and bars and do stuff with their friends. Once people have children, they tend to invest more in their home environment and value good schools and safe neighborhoods. As we get even older, we may be more concerned about climate, or our proximity to family members. This is an ongoing conversation that you should be having with the people you love. Finding someone who wants the same lifestyle as you, and enjoys the same activities as you, certainly makes life easier. But we know plenty of creative couples who have figured out how to honor and encourage their partners to enjoy their Happy Places, even when they are not their own.

66 Where a person lives determines their level of happiness more than any other factor. 99

DAN BUETTNER

Amy's Story

Amy attended one of our women's leadership retreats just after leaving her job as an elementary school teacher and starting her own company called Women's Radical Pursuits (WRP). WRP brings women on mountain biking excursions to international destinations and encourages them to do life-changing work on themselves. They challenge their bodies by riding tough trails while also challenging what's happening on the inside of themselves, such as confronting limiting beliefs and inner critics. WHERE matters to Amy – exploring the mountains and traveling to new cultures feeds her soul. For Amy, WHERE is not just a geographical place. It is also what she does when she is there, and how it makes her feel. Amy says, "My Z is being in the mountains – places that make me feel free, happy, and connected." When reflecting on what it feels like when she's bombing down a mountain on her bike, she says, "I come alive! It brings out the best in me. I love the climb, I love the challenge, but I know it's all about enjoying the journey."

Amy's journey has had its detours for sure. In 2020 the pandemic forced a two-year pause in her adventures, so she used that time to reflect and consider her options. Through that reflection, she discovered a way to continue fueling her love for the communities that had touched her life. She partnered with Project Bike Love, Every Pedal MTB, and Coyote Adventures to provide bikes to kids in the villages in Mexico where she worked. Through fundraising efforts, she and her partners raised $10,000 and donated hundreds of bikes! All Women's Radical Pursuits trips will now donate a portion of their profits back to the community to keep fueling this project, spreading the joy of biking to others.

All of this has been possible because Amy chases her dreams. When she isn't happy about where she is in her alphabet, she gives herself permission to change. Her company has uniquely combined her passion (WHAT), with her purpose (WHY), and her WHERE to build the company and life of her dreams! Shifting gears is a challenge, but Amy has been able to move from the letter "D" to the letter "U" in only a few years time. And now she is helping others do the same!

Watch Amy's Story

GAUGE CHECK: HOW CLEAR ARE YOU FEELING ABOUT YOUR WHERE NOW?

We hope the exercises and stories in this section have helped you gain more clarity about your WHERE. These insights will help you focus on creating the lifestyle you want, so you can have the happiness you deserve.

Draw a line that indicates your current level of clarity after reading *Finding Your WHERE.*

I know WHERE my Happy Place is and I am intentionally navigating my life toward these experiences and destinations.

UNCLEAR   CLEAR

REFLECTING ON FINDING YOUR WHERE

Questions We Explored

- Where is my Happy Place?

- What is my ideal lifestyle right now?

- What am I doing when I feel most myself or most alive?

Through these exercises and your personal reflection, we hope you are feeling clearer and more confident about finding your Happy Place – or your WHERE. We hope reflecting on your vision of an ideal day and the images that surrounded you, have inspired you to continue to intentionally navigate your life toward your WHERE.

Now, it's time for the section you have probably been waiting for, because we all spend so much of our lives doing it. We will help you answer the age-old question: "What do you want to be when you grow up?"

Let's go find your WHAT.

Chapter 6:

FINDING
YOUR WHAT

FINDING YOUR WHAT
Questions to Explore

- What would I do if I could do anything professionally?

- What am I doing when I'm in my professional "sweet spot?"

- What are the unique strengths and skills that I bring to the world?

Finding Your WHAT will focus mostly on your professional career, but it may also reveal hobbies that would give you pleasure and fulfillment without a paycheck – volunteer work, home improvement projects, or creative writing could all be components of your WHAT. How you make a living is not always how you make a life. Think about Andy and his music! Most career development workshops focus solely on helping you figure out your strengths, or how to demonstrate a more executive presence, so you can land a bigger job. We see your WHAT as a source of energy, or a thief of it – it can rob you of your precious time and well-being if it isn't the right for you. Finding your "dream job" requires you to fully appreciate your WHY, WHO, and WHERE at least as much as your WHAT if you can make smarter tradeoffs in your life.

Abbi's Story

Abbi created a life she thought she wanted. In her early 20s she went to cosmetology school, became a reality TV star, got married, and started a family. But somewhere along the way, she fell into a slump – she felt like she was losing herself. She was struggling in her marriage, struggling financially, and suffering from post-partum depression. She talks about a moment when she pulled the blankets up over her head in bed and thought, "Is this it? What is wrong with me?" She felt like she was at the very beginning of her alphabet and could not even begin to imagine her Z. "I didn't even dream. I thought maybe we'd have an average life – and I am not an average person!" She was searching for something to bring her "sparkle" back.

Then, along came LimeLife – a network marketing company that sells cosmetics. What started as an interest – something she just loved to do, playing with makeup – grew into a calling. In her first month with LimeLife, she earned what she had been making sitting behind a desk at her father's insurance company. In the years that followed, she grew her business into the millions and her team into the thousands. Her passion shifted from selling makeup to empowering thousands of women to follow their entrepreneurial dreams – coaching them on how to grow their business, become more financially secure, and enjoy their time at home raising a family. Her desire to change her own life eventually changed the lives of countless other women.

Abbi started with a strong WHAT but it was her WHY that kept her going. "My WHY evolved over time. At first, this business was just for me. Then I wanted to change my family's life. Then I saw what I was creating, and how I was changing other people's lives. How I was inspiring them to come on this journey and finding self-worth. So then my WHY became: I'm going to change the world. This is bigger than me … LimeLife is just the vehicle."

We share Abbi's story as a WHAT story because she truly found her "sweet spot" – the intersection between what she loved to do, what she was good at, what the world needed, and what she could be paid for. Abbi is clear about every element of her alphabet and she is racing toward her Z.

Watch Abbi's Story

66 Everyone in life has a calling. And your real job in life is to figure out as soon as possible what that is, who you were meant to be, and honoring that in the best possible way for yourself. **99**

OPRAH WINFREY

FINDING YOUR WHAT

You cannot overestimate the impact of a fulfilling career on your happiness. We invite you to consider the workplace as a container for realizing what you are capable of. Your job fuels your lifestyle. Your career can provide meaning and relationships and take you on amazing adventures. Once you know who you are, and what you want, you will seek work that provides a highway toward your ideal life.

Finding Your WHAT is important because, on average, human beings spend one-third of their lifetime at work, making work a core component of life itself. So let's get this part right!

WHAT IS IKIGAI?

The Japanese have a phrase called *Ikigai*, which translated directly means "a reason for being." It is also loosely translated as "the thing that you live for" or "the reason for which you wake up in the morning." Ikigai is visualized as the intersection of four elements coming together:

1. **What you are good at**
2. **What you love to do**
3. **What the world needs, and …**
4. **What you can get paid for**

The combination of any two elements reveals the difference between finding your profession, vocation, passion, and mission. At the heart of it is your Ikigai, your "sweet spot," which is the goal of *Finding Your WHAT.*

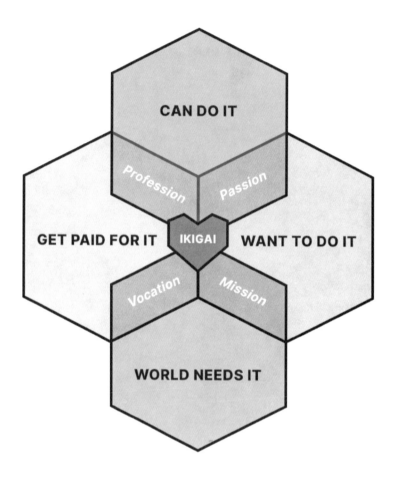

According to Wikipedia, Ikigai is used to indicate the source of value in one's life or the things that make life worthwhile. It also refers to the mental and spiritual circumstances under which individuals feel that their lives are valuable. It's not necessarily linked to one's financial status. This last part is key, as the financial piece of our work life is often what drives our decision making when presented with new opportunities. This model requires a new definition of "success" that may not align with the traditional cultural markers you are using.

Let's look at each of these four elements as "lenses" you can use to examine your WHAT.

1. **CAN DO (Skills/Strengths) – Work I am capable of doing**

2. **WANT TO DO (Will/Desire) – Work I enjoy doing**

3. **WORLD NEEDS (Demand) – Work the world needs someone to do**

4. **GET PAID (Market) – Work the world will pay someone to do**

So often, when people get stuck or lost in their careers, it is because they find themselves doing "Can Do" work versus their "Want to Do" work. "Can Do" work is work you are capable of doing, but it may not align with your passions or feel meaningful to you. Candyce CAN create beautiful PowerPoint pages, but spending her life behind a computer is a waste of her actual talents and gifts. The danger of doing too much "Can Do" work is that you spend your career being comfortable; repeatedly doing the same thing you are already good at – (*And guess what? It tends to be something other people hate doing*!) – instead of learning and growing into the work you could truly enjoy and find fulfilling. The intersection between WHAT you are good at (your knowledge and strengths) and WHAT you love to do, is where passion lies.

Imagine your boss says that there is an opportunity for you to step up and lead a team for the first time in your career. How do you evaluate this type of decision? How do you know it's right for you? Is this something you **CAN DO** – meaning you currently possess the skills, knowledge, and strength needed to lead people? Or would this be your first opportunity doing something like this? Instead of calling "leadership" a weakness, let's think about it as a potential "weak strength." A "weak strength" is something you have never done, but there is a high probability you would be great at it. A colleague of our once described a "weak strength" as "pigment under your skin." It is just lying there below the surface, but you won't know it is there, or how much you have of it, until you expose it to the sun. Some people have a lot of pigment when it comes to leading teams and some individuals will burn in the sunlight of leadership. But you don't know until you expose yourself to it! Too many people, especially women, read a job description and stop themselves from applying because they don't meet 100% of the qualifications listed. Jobs should provide growth, so grab your sunglasses and try leading!

Now let's switch up this scenario a little by providing more context – that leadership role your boss wants you to consider requires you to lead a large team who are going through a lot of change. You know that change management and public speaking will be a core part of the position. These are not your strengths; in fact, those things are true weaknesses of yours. You don't have those skills AND you are not interested in developing those skills. In that case, managing this large team might not be the right move for you. You might be better suited to lead a small team your first time out. Never declare your major in a zone of weakness. If you are bad at math, don't spend your career in accounting. If you hate public speaking, don't take a role that constantly puts you in the spotlight.

If you major in your strengths, the unique world-class capabilities that differentiate you from most people, you will be more successful. Let's say you are a super clear-headed problem solver in emotionally charged situations. You have noticed that you are naturally better at level-headed thinking than most of the people you work with. You're not sure why, but it's just easier for you to handle pressure and stress than other people you work with. That's an insight into your strengths. Lean into that. You should probably pursue roles that need someone like you because it is a differentiator. If you are a great public speaker, that is a rare skill. If you are able to write communications that people say "WOW!" about, pay attention! These could be your moneymakers! Identify the most differentiated skills you have and find the roles that need you.

You should also consider what you want to do. The "WANT TO" factor is about the degree to which you desire the work. Some career paths are worth the required trade-offs – you might be willing to make less money, commute farther, work longer hours, or even relocate for the chance to have a job that provides more of what you want in life. Look at your Values! If a role can give you more of your Top 5 Values, wouldn't you want to go for it? Imagine yourself doing work that fills up your Values bucket day after day – providing an abundance of the impact, or freedom, or fun, or growth that you crave. That is how it feels to find the work you WANT TO do. The benefits seem to always outweigh the trade-offs.

We hope you are thinking about the type of careers and tasks that might fall into your WANT TO work – these can be hobbies or pastimes, or tasks where you get lost in the flow of enjoyment. Things you would choose to do just for fun or fulfillment. Increasingly, we see people turning their pastimes or zones of genius into careers – from crafting, cooking, decorating, traveling, dancing, shopping, and collecting – thousands of TikTokers, Ebayers, Etsy Shop Owners, and Instagrammers have turned their passions and strengths into income.

If you are built for a more conventional career, notice the type of work you raise your hand for, or look forward to, on your calendar. Notice when you feel most confident and content at work. It may be mentoring younger professionals, or talking with clients, or solving complex problems in Excel, or creating something that doesn't exist yet. Find the elements of work that fill your tank, and then find a role that allows you to do more of that in a day.

The "World Needs It" and You Will "Get Paid" for It

The difference between a pastime and a vocation are the last two lenses – is there a need for someone to do this work in the world, and can you get paid for doing it? Let's start with the *world needs it*. Are there companies currently hiring for the type of job you want? At different times in our lives, we have seen the job market constrain and expand. What is the market like right now for the type of work you want to do? Also consider the reality of where you live and the number of roles available there. Say you want to be the Plant Manager of the one factory in your hometown. There is only one Plant Manager role available and it is currently filled by a 45-year-old man who is not planning on retiring anytime soon. Is this an opportunity you are willing to wait for, or do you need to move somewhere they need a Plant Manager?

If there is an intersection of CAN DO work (You are capable of being a Plant Manager), WANT TO work (Being a Plant Manager would be fulfilling for you), and there is a NEED for one two hours away, it may be worth moving or commuting for.

We have intentionally avoided the topic of "money" so far, because our experience tells us too many people start and end their evaluation of a job with one question, "How much does it pay?" This makes sense, because only a few people in the world are in a position of volunteering their lifetime in pursuit of something that won't pay the bills. But salary is not a telescope – don't solely evaluate a job opportunity by looking at the compensation package. Instead, we would encourage you to find something that meets most of the other criteria we've laid out and then ask yourself if you will make ENOUGH money in that role to have the life you want. Enough to keep a roof over your head, food in your belly, and enjoy the lifestyle you desire. This is a shift in thinking, to be sure! Most Americans do not have an "Enough" mindset, they have a "More" mindset. More money would always be better, right? Well … not necessarily! We know a lot of people who say yes to a big paycheck but their life is filled with stress and their relationships are suffering. Or people who have all the money in the world and still feel deeply unfulfilled. We are not suggesting that money doesn't matter – in fact, we believe money actually CAN buy happiness if it is invested in the things that make you happy. Spending money on vacations, or living in a safe neighborhood, or paying for your gym membership, are things that can make every hour you spend at work feel worthwhile. But buying designer handbags or fancy cars might feel meaningless to you personally so they are not worth working overtime to afford. In an ideal world, the job you CAN DO and WANT TO DO pays well and companies are clamoring to hire you for that work.

FINDING YOUR "SWEET SPOT"

There will be times when your boss, or somebody else at work says, "We really need someone who can do this thing, and you're really good at doing it. We would love for you to say yes to this opportunity because we need someone like you." That is really flattering, isn't it? So you say, "Alright, I can do that for you." (*Look at you being the hero!*) But what if the job isn't one you are personally excited about? Are you willing to take one for the team – fix this big problem, support this big project, or manage this big change – as a deposit into your organization's growth account? Or is this another situation where you are being flattered into a "CAN DO" job that you don't really want? Saying *yes* to these "CAN DO" jobs can lead to a slog of workdays strung together, and lunch hours spent looking for your dream job online. This is what happens when you leave the "WANT TO" part out. Taking this job might earn you points with your boss, but it could be a big withdrawal from your own happiness.

On the flipside, there could be a situation where you say, "Oh, I want that job! But I have no experience doing something like that. Heck, I don't even know if I'm capable of doing that!" And your boss might decide to take a chance on you and give you a bigger job than you've ever had before! What happens when you take a job like that? You might work more hours getting up to speed but you are undoubtedly learning and growing. That is when the company is making a deposit in YOUR growth account. Alternating between you making deposits in a company, and the company making deposits in you, prevents resentment and burnout.

If you dream of owning a business making earwax candles, but you can't find anybody who wants one or will pay for one, that dream may not be worth exploring. You might need to find a different type of candle to burn. Maybe you want to be a dog walker and spend your days outside hiking and playing with furry best friends, but you don't think anyone would really PAY YOU to do that. Do you *know* that, or do you *think* that? A dream is worth pursuing fully until the world proves it can't be your reality. Don't give up before you even make a flyer. Finding your Ikigai, or your sweet spot, is the goal. Have you ever done a job or managed a project that placed you in your sweet spot? Do you remember how great it felt to go to work with a pep in your step and feel excited for Monday? If you think dog walking could be your Ikigai, start doing it as a pastime until it can become your profession.

As with the rest of the elements in *Finding Your Z*, as your career grows and your life changes, your "sweet spot" will shift. You could start a job square in the middle, but then something changes and you are no longer comfortable with the trade-offs you made. Maybe you have a baby, and that 45-minute commute just isn't working for your family. That's when it's time to find the next letter in your alphabet. It's time to get your life back in the sweet spot.

DO MORE OF WHAT YOU LOVE

Some of you are already clear about the work you want to do more of in your life, but some may still feel a bit dazed and confused – we'd like to offer you a few "Career Coaching Tips" that have been refined through coaching numerous individuals facing major career decisions.

FIND YOUR FLOW: Consider the tasks you find yourself doing where it feels like no time has passed at all. You realize you could do it all day long and not feel tired or bored – it could be talking to people, or reading books, or creating and building things. The field of positive psychology refers to the sensation of time passing quickly as being in a state of "flow." It is also referred to as being "in the zone," and according to Mihaly Csikszentmihalyi, one of the co-founders of positive psychology, it is a mental state of operation in which a person becomes fully immersed in something they are doing. It is described as energized focus, where you feel full involvement and enjoyment in the process of completing an activity. **What are you doing when you find yourself in "flow?"** This is important because research suggests that your brain is wired perfectly for these types of tasks!

ALLOW YOURSELF TO DREAM: Another way to think about it is to ask yourself: "What would I do if I could do anything?" If there were no constraints like money, time, energy, capabilities, or risks, what would you LOVE to do? What do you imagine yourself doing that would fill you with gratitude and joy? Our friend Staci dreams of owning a coffee shop and baking all day. Candyce's daughter dreams of traveling all over the world reviewing restaurants and hotels. Do you let yourself dream? **Do you allow yourself to imagine what you would ideally do, or are you fixated on the reality of what you currently do?** Let yourself dream. There are insights that can help you find a new pastime, if not a new job to apply for.

KNOW WHY PEOPLE LOVE YOU: Guess what? People think you are really great…at certain things. They come to you for that superpower you have – your advice, your skill, your strengths – because they see it as your genius. **What do people come to you for?** What are the qualities that people praise you for? What do people compliment you on? If you can't see it for yourself, look at yourself through someone else's eyes.

 DEFINE SUCCESS FOR YOURSELF: *Finding your WHAT may require you to ignore the cultural paradigms of success that surround you. There is not a prescribed formula for what success is that you cannot challenge.* If you did not graduate from college, find someone who you think is successful that also did not go to college. If your parents were workaholics – who went into their offices before the sun rose and took conference calls on vacation – know that you do not need to sacrifice your weekends to succeed. Candyce and Michelle have both achieved a level of financial success that is apparent to the outside world – we live in nice homes, we take vacations, we have beautiful families, and we have jobs that are deeply fulfilling – but we also have flexibility with the balance of our work and life. Find the evidence that challenges your assumptions about what success is, and how to reach it. It will free you from believing that there is only one path to happiness.

In 2021, it was reported that Americans are the most depressed, medicated, stressed out, and disconnected people in the world. And yet many were reaching new levels of wealth and had access to more options and conveniences than any generation before them. None of that netted out to happiness.

WHAT doesn't always have to be the thing that provides an income. It can just be something you love to do, something that gives you pleasure and purpose. In some instances, making it a job would actually take the joy out of it. Deciding to volunteer at your church or at the local pet shelter – could be a great way to invest your free time. If you value "Impact" it most certainly will. Once you know what you love to do, make the time and space for it in your life. This is WHAT will get you closer to your Z.

EXERCISE 14:
Your Career Inventory

This exercise tends to be everyone's favorite in the live workshops we lead. We typically do it as a card sorting game, which is hard to replicate in a book. But we will give it a shot!

The Career Inventory is our favorite way to help people answer the age-old question: "What do you want to be when you grow up?" It will also help you decide which doors you want to close for good in your life. **This is a multi-step process! Set aside at least an hour to complete it.**

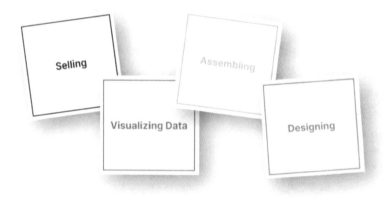

STEP 1: Download the "Career Inventory" exercise from our website using the QR Code provided. *For best results, print the PDF 2-sided and in full color. Single sided printing in black & white will also work though less ideal. The PDF is free to download and includes:*

1. Directions for completing Steps 1-3 of this activity

2. A placemat for sorting the cards into four categories

3. Career Cards: On each card is a word that represents a category of work people are paid to do in the world. You will read each card and determine to what extent you "CAN DO" this type of work, and to what extent you "WANT TO DO" this type of work. *You will need to cut the cards into individual squares to complete this exercise.*

STEP 2: Look at each word on the cards and determine if you "CAN DO" this type of work *(you are competent and capable of doing this)*, and if you "WANT TO" do this type of work *(you find this fulfilling and enjoyable)*. You get to interpret the meaning of each card for yourself. If two cards are describing the same thing in your mind, just put both cards in the same pile. **You will need to place every card (or word) in one of the four boxes before you can move forward.**

SAMPLE CAREER CARD INVENTORY

I CAN DO this well
but
I DON'T LOVE to do this

Visualizing Data

CAN DO WORK

I CAN DO this well
and
I LOVE TO to do this

Selling

MY SWEET SPOT

I CAN'T DO this well
and
I DON'T LOVE to do this

Assembling

AVOID IF POSSIBLE!

I CAN'T DO this well
but
I WOULD LOVE to do this

Designing

WANT TO WORK

STEP 3: Once you have categorized all of the cards into the four boxes, notice which box has the most words, and which box has the fewest words. Count the total number of words you put into each box.

BOX 1: _____ **BOX 2:** _____ **BOX 3:** _____ **BOX 4:** _____

Does anything surprise you about your results?

_____

_____

What stands out already?

_____

_____

If the top row of the chart is full of cards (*Boxes 1 & 2*) it suggests you might be incredibly capable and confident. You may have already had a wide range of career experiences.

If you are earlier on in your career, you may underestimate your capabilities and have a lot of words in the bottom boxes (*Boxes 3 & 4*). Or maybe your results are surprisingly even? Just be curious at this point, not judgmental.

STEP 4: Now we will look at what each box is telling you, starting with the box you should avoid.

BOX #3: I CANNOT DO THIS WELL, AND I DO NOT ENJOY DOING IT

The type of work you placed in Box #3 describes the work you find least fulfilling – we call it the "Avoid if Possible" Box. Do NOT ignore this box! In fact, commit these words to memory! If you read a job description containing a number of these words, run in the opposite direction! Do not pass GO, and do not collect $200. Starting today, you can confidently say *no* to these things – they are, "What you are *not* going to be when you grow up." Allow the words in this box to represent your "Closed Doors" which may generate a certain sense of relief in those individuals who feel overwhelmed by all of the choices in their lives.

BOX #2: I CAN DO THIS WELL, AND I ENJOY DOING IT

In the opposite corner, the opposite is true. These are the things you are good at and you enjoy doing – we call this box your "Sweet Spot!" Move toward the roles and opportunities that allow you to do this stuff more often. This type of work will not only be more fulfilling, but you will likely enjoy more success when you are doing it. Put these words into your favorite search engines and see what type of roles pop up! Are these words available in a profession that interest you? Are some of them hobbies? How does your current job align, or not align, with the words in this box? Hold onto these "cards," because they are the key to your dream job!

BOX #1: I CAN DO THIS WELL, BUT I DON'T ENJOY IT

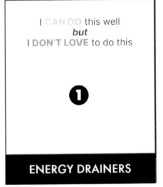

These words represent your "Can Do" work, and they can be real "Energy Drainers." Review the words you placed in this box. This type of work may be what other people want you to do, but notice that you said you don't enjoy doing it. Some elements of this work in your day-to-day life is fine, but if the majority of your workday is spent on these tasks you'll go home feeling unsatisfied and deeply exhausted. This is not where your passions lie. Minimize the amount of time you spend in this area to maximize your happiness at work.

BOX #4: I CANNOT DO THIS WELL, BUT I WOULD ENJOY LEARNING IT

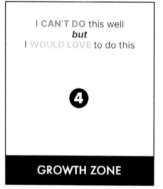

Review the cards you placed in the lower right-hand corner – this is your "Growth Zone." Seek out elements of this work in your next role or practice these skills in your free time. These are your opportunities for growth! You may find this work challenging, but rewarding. We suggest finding roles that have 3 to 4 words in your Sweet Spot and 1 to 2 words in your Growth Zone if you want to stay in a job for more than 12 months.

STEP 5: *Narrowing It Down.*

Now that we have looked at all of the words in each category, it is time to narrow things down to identify your next role. **Select 5 CARDS from your "Sweet Spot" pile and 1 CARD from your Growth Zone to describe your dream job. Which 6 cards did you pick? Write down those words here:**

1. **My TOP 5 "Sweet Spot" Cards:**

   _____

   _____

2. **My #1 "Growth Zone" (what I am most interested in learning / developing):**

   _____

   _____

Could these 6 words be describing your next dream job? If not, what's missing?

_____

_____

What are your key takeaways from this *Finding Your WHAT* exercise?

_____

_____

WHAT DO THE COLORS MEAN?

As you may have guessed, the colors of each card represent broader categories of work. Look up the color of your Top 6 words. Is there is a TREND? Which color did you primarily select?

- **BLACK** – If you selected primarily BLACK cards, you enjoy working with People. Working from home, or in isolation, will deplete your energy and enjoyment at work. Seek out opportunities where you will be a part of a team, talk with clients or customers, and be in a community with others.

- **PURPLE** – If you selected primarily PURPLE cards, you enjoy working with Data & Information! You like thinking deeply about things, and digging into complex questions by researching, analyzing, and calculating until you find the answers. You love the accuracy and clarity that information can provide, because you know how to organize and use it to your advantage.

- **TEAL** – If you selected primarily TEAL cards, you should find a career working with Product & Things. You enjoy using both your head and hands to work on new products, objects, or results. Careers in engineering, production, construction, or marketing will allow you to physically manifest something that is a tangible result of your efforts.

- **RED** – If you selected primarily RED cards you are an Idea person! Consider roles that allow you think big, be creative, and explore new ways of working. You will enjoy being on the front-end of projects, but may lose steam when it is time to get into the details. You are energized by questions, such as: "How might we…?" or "What if we…?" The bigger and more groundbreaking the idea, the more engaged you will be.

Most people select words that are a blend of colors, not just one. We hope these colors and "cards" provided you with important insights into the careers you would find most fulfilling.

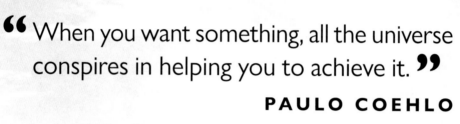

> **"** When you want something, all the universe conspires in helping you to achieve it. **"**
>
> **PAULO COEHLO**

The Bishop Brothers' Story

Tyler and Timmy Bishop have a special connection to *Finding Your Z*. We met Tyler in a hotel lobby during our first writer's retreat. That morning we had been brainstorming about how to create a "platform" for our book that would attract our future readers. We recognized that telling people's stories would be a really engaging strategy for helping people understand the concepts of *Finding Your Z*. We thought it would be great to find a videographer who could help us film people telling their stories so we could share them on social media. Problem was, neither of us knew a videographer.

As we stepped off the hotel elevator to go to lunch, we saw a young man in a chair with what appeared to be a large video camera next to him. We approached him, and after a short conversation, found out that his name was Tyler and he was at the hotel filming a wedding – a side gig he had recently started because he loved videography. His real job was working in IT at a corporation in Minneapolis. We asked Tyler if he would consider creating *Finding Your Z* videos for us, an opportunity he jumped into with both feet! *(Whoa! Did we just MANIFEST this moment or what?)*

Tyler traveled thousands of miles with us, bombed down mountains on a mountain bike, and worked endless hours editing footage to tell the best stories possible. He became our friend, and we became his cheerleaders. We knew he was talented, really talented, but he needed to bet on himself and take the leap from his corporate job if ever wanted to realize his Z. Tyler is a responsible person – he understood his parents' investment in his education and didn't want to let them down. As parents ourselves, we knew his mom and dad would not want him to suffer in a cubical when he was born to be creative. As suspected, they fully supported him and he resigned a few months later.

Tyler was already in the business of dreaming when we met him. He regularly got together with a group of his male friends at a local restaurant to talk about their goals and hold each other accountable for reaching them. They called themselves the *Dreamers*. One day they invited us to a Dreamer meeting – *the first females to ever get invited, thank you very much* – where we met Tyler's brother Timmy. Timmy had ridden a Greyhound bus overnight to be there with us. He was about to graduate from the University of Wisconsin Madison with a degree in Marketing and was feeling unsure about what he wanted to do next. We asked Timmy to join our *Finding Your Z* Band and oversee our social media and marketing.

When we had to put *Finding Your Z* on "pause" due to the pandemic, these young men did not stop chasing their dreams. The universe brought us together at the perfect moment, but we were only meant to travel together for a short distance. Where they went next, was unbelievable!

Tyler created his own production company so he could continue to tell stories through videos. He was offered some amazing opportunities – including going on an African safari in Botswana to shoot a documentary about climate change and water conservation. His brother Timmy started dreaming HARD and created detailed goals and plans for his life. One of his goals was to join the Dream Team with Charlie "Rocket" Jabaley – a music mogul turned social entrepreneur who was traveling the country on a bus called *The Dream Machine*. When Timmy learned that Charlie was going to be touring only a few hours away from Minneapolis, he convinced Tyler to go meet him at a podcast studio – and the rest is history! They joined the Dream Machine Tour, and today the Bishop Brothers travel the country raising money and making dreams come true for thousands of people. They are leading a movement alongside Charlie and the rest of his Dream Team, and inspiring other young people to make a difference in the world. Tyler's videos have now been liked by millions of people around the world on Instagram and TikTok – including Steve Harvey and Oprah Winfrey! Timmy is now the COO of the movement and spends his days truly changing people's lives. It all began with him setting goals and not being afraid to dream. We are amazed by the Bishop Brothers, and proud to call them our friends. We can't wait to see what they do next!

❝ You can only be truly accomplished at something you love. **❞**

MAYA ANGELOU

GAUGE CHECK: HOW CLEAR ARE YOU FEELING ABOUT YOUR WHAT NOW?

We hope the exercises and stories in this section have helped you gain more clarity about your WHAT. These insights will help you focus on finding your dream job and do more fulfilling work in the world.

Draw a line that indicates your current level of clarity after reading *Finding Your WHAT*.

I know WHAT I should spend my time doing and what I should not spend my time doing. I can clearly articulate my professional "sweet spot" to others.

UNCLEAR   **CLEAR**

REFLECTING ON FINDING YOUR WHAT
Questions We Explored

- What would I do if I could do anything professionally?

- What am I doing when I'm in my professional "sweet spot?"

- What are the unique strengths and skills that I bring to the world?

Through the exercises and stories we have shared, we hope you are feeling clearer and more confident about what you want to do in the world, and that you will go find your WHAT. Through reflecting on each of the four elements of Ikigai – work you CAN DO, work you WANT TO DO, work the WORLD NEEDS done, and work you can GET PAID for, you should feel clearer about what your dream job looks like at this point in your life. It is important to take ACTION and not just let your dream remain a dream. You need to get closer to your ideal life.

Now, let's meet that little voice inside your head telling you that your dream is crazy.

Let's go talk to YOUR BACKSEAT DRIVER!

Chapter 7:

YOUR BACKSEAT DRIVER

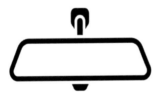

YOUR BACKSEAT DRIVER

Questions to Explore

1. How does your inner dialogue impact your ability to reach goals and pursue your ideal life?

2. What are the situations that activate your inner critic (aka your Backseat Driver)?

3. In those situations, what does your Backseat Driver say to you?

4. How can you manage your Backseat Driver?

Clark's Story

Our coaching client, Clark, literally felt like he had two different creatures living inside his head.

One creature he called **Bob the Blob** – a very lazy, unmotivated sort with no passion, no energy, and no dreams for his future. Whenever Clark would try something new, Bob would proverbially whisper in his ear, "You're going to look like an idiot" or "Why would you even bother?" Bob the Blob whispered terrible, terrible things to him. Through our coaching, Clark unpacked the source of those sound bites and realized they were a manifestation of things he had heard his Dad tell him growing up. His Dad whispered words like this into his life and they became the voices Clark listened to inside his head. Clark wanted desperately to replace Bob the Blob with a very different character – one that pumped him up, made him feel capable and inspired. So we suggested he create a character he wanted to listen to instead of Bob the Blob. Actually, we told him to get out some colored pencils and draw him.

The character he created was called **Super Bob** and he was the polar opposite of Bob the Blob. Super Bob looked at himself in the mirror and said things like, "Hello Gorgeous." He puffed out his chest, put his hands on his hips, and held his chin up high. To rid himself of the dreaded Bob the Blob and channel his inner Super Bob, every day Clark looked in the mirror and manifested his inner Superhero. He created an entirely different soundtrack, which made a huge difference in his energy and mindset. Super Bob became the antidote to Bob the Blob and things started to change around him.

Do you have a Bob the Blob, or a similar character, taking up space in your head – crushing your dreams before you even begin? The answer to that question is – *we all do*! This is the voice of the inner critic, or what we like to call the **Backseat Driver**. Let's take some time to explore how your Backseat Driver sabotages you by proverbially tapping you on the shoulder and whispering limiting beliefs in your ear.

 Your Backseat Driver may not like that you are reading *Finding Your Z.*

YOUR BACKSEAT DRIVER

By this point in the book, you know your WHAT, your WHERE, your WHO and your WHY. You are ready to kick it into high gear and head down the road to Z. You are inspired and full of hope and promise – you have all of the tools in your trunk and you have an action plan to reach the next letters in the alphabet. Then … nothing. NOTHING. What happens to us when we start to try new things, take a risk, or do something we would not normally do? We get scared. We confront habit loops. We start doubting ourselves and our abilities. We tell ourselves it's just a silly dream and it's time to get our head out of the clouds and go back to our safe, comfortable lives. We beat ourselves up for being selfish by wanting more than what we already have because aren't we "#Blessed" enough?! We berate ourselves for spending time on dream chasing when everyone else clearly needs our attention and energy more.

All of these thoughts are the *low-down dirty work* of the Backseat Driver. If you think the WHO in your life has influence on whether or not you're successful, they have relatively no power compared to the Backseat Driver that lives between your ears. That voice can say some of the most cruel, outlandish, shameful, hurtful things – more than anyone else in your life would ever dare utter to you.

The Backseat Driver sounds like your own fears and insecurities, but the voices are often a combination of soundbites from other people you have interacted with over the course of your life. Maybe a parent, or a trusted adult, coach, or teacher who limited your choices or said you couldn't do something you set out to do. Maybe you were made to feel small or stupid. Maybe people lovingly sabotaged you by trying to keep you safe, warning you to avoid risk and danger.

Research suggests that most Backseat Driver voices form in our heads between the ages of two and five, and are fully formed by the time we are eight years old! Eight years old! We are letting eight-year-olds talk us out of achieving our dreams. How do you feel about having an eight-year-old, and their lack of life experience and wisdom running your life?

Your Backseat Driver is a tricky beast, because it sounds just like your own voice. It can be difficult to separate the voice in your head from your own beliefs, dreams, and ambitions. It's easy to think they are one in the same. The danger with this is that the purpose of your Backseat Driver is to keep you safe, to keep you small. Anything the Backseat Driver perceives as a risk or out of your comfort zone is fair game for criticism. Their purpose is to maintain the status quo, and you've probably already figured out that *Finding Your Z* is not about maintaining the status quo! Our guess is that isn't what you want either, or you wouldn't have bothered to plunk down your hard-earned cash for this book.

CHECKING YOUR REARVIEW MIRROR

One way to activate your Backseat Driver is "checking the rearview mirror." Basically, when your eyes are on the rearview mirror instead of the road ahead, you are ruminating on past mistakes or missteps. We bring these regrets into our present lives even though we can't change what happened. How many times have you set out to try something new but automatically recalled a painful experience or failure from your past that stopped you cold?

For example:

- One of our daughters fell off a scooter and was severely hurt at age 9. She is currently in high school but still refuses to get back on a scooter or ride a bike.

- Our colleague had a terrible first date after subscribing to Bumble, and now swears all online dating is a scam.

- We are coaching a person who once turned bright red during a big work presentation when she was 25 years old. She just turned down *another* promotion for fear of having to present in front of Senior Leaders in that role. She is currently 47.

Certainly, we should glance in our rearview mirror…briefly. It serves a purpose for us to learn and grow so that we don't continually make the same mistakes. However, when our failures or mistakes become our entire focus, we miss what's ahead on the horizon.

There is value in granting yourself the grace to own up to your mistakes and failures but not allow them define you. When you let go of what's in the rearview mirror, you free yourself from the burdens of your past. There is a quote by Mike Rusch we love that addresses this concept: "Grace means that all of your mistakes now serve a purpose, instead of serving shame." Do you feel the weight lift from your shoulders when you hear that phrase? It doesn't mean that your mistakes didn't happen or that you shouldn't be aware of them. It just means that they shouldn't hold you back – quite the opposite, actually. Your mistakes and failures should fuel your action forward, because now that you know better, you can do better. There are all kinds of examples available demonstrating how some of the most successful people in the world – Oprah, Walt Disney, Michael Jordan, and JK Rowling, just to name a few – failed spectacularly on their way to achieving astronomical success. What if they'd allowed their own Rearview Mirrors to get in their way? Can you imagine a world without Mickey Mouse or Harry Potter?

IMPOSTER SYNDROME

Another activator for the Backseat Driver is something called the *Imposter Syndrome*. The Imposter Syndrome is a specific narrative that taunts extraordinarily talented people – typically someone uniquely positioned as an expert in their field, or someone who has reached a new pinnacle in their career. Despite a clear demonstration of competence, some people feel like they are a fraud and fooling everyone. These are generally high-achieving people who struggle to accept their accomplishments as real – they believe their achievements are the result of luck or coincidence instead of hard work and expertise. They torment themselves worrying about being "found out" by people realizing they aren't as capable as everyone thinks they are. The inner voice can sound like, "If you only knew" and it often results in people becoming guarded and closed off from others.

If this resonates with you, the Imposter Syndrome may be making an appearance. Getting to Z is as much about enjoying the fruits of your labor and success as it is about achieving them in the first place. If you continually don't accept your accomplishments as your own, how much do you think you are enjoying your life?

One way to combat and defeat the Backseat Driver is to examine your inner monologue and separate it from yourself – for example, draw a cartoon character that embodies your Backseat Driver. By objectifying it, and writing down what it actually says to you, you can challenge and change it. You are rarely the origin of the voices – those words were first spoken by another person, or society, or both. You choosing to believe in the voices is what gives them the power. Recognizing you have the power to change the soundtrack creates a moment of choice. It allows you to say, "I don't believe that about myself, so it no longer has power over me."

Let's manifest your Backseat Driver now by giving it a name – ideally a name you don't like or that represents a negative persona in your real life. Get creative! Some examples we've heard are: *Rob* (because he's robbin' your dreams), *Ursula* (or other Disney villains), *Regina George* (get out the BURN BOOK!), or the names of someone's parents or bad bosses. For the sake of an example in this book, we will call the Backseat Driver "Irene." (Our apologies if that's your name, but Michelle had a crotchety great-aunt named Irene who was unhappy with pretty much everything in life). When you encounter a situation that activates your Backseat Driver, you can simply acknowledge it and say to yourself, "Not today, Irene! I hear you but I'm not listening!" or mentally flip Irene The Bird, if you're feeling so bold!

If you don't want your Backseat Driver bossing you around for the rest of your life, there is a proven way to manage them. Step #1 is noticing *when* your Inner-Irene gets activated. These moments are called your *triggers*. We know that the word trigger, well, triggers some people. In fact, our editor suggested we remove it from the book. But it is a term frequently used in neuroscience to describe a stimulus that activates a mental reaction, which is the point we are trying to make. Your inner critic switches on involuntarily when you are put in certain situations. It may happen when you are learning something new or acting "irresponsibly." It might happen when you are trying to break a habit – like going on a diet, trying to spend less money, or trying to control your temper. The Backseat Driver reminds you of all the times in your life when you have not succeeded, when things didn't work out, and whispers "Wouldn't it feel good to just curl back up in your comfort zone, eat the cake, and shop on Amazon instead of all this TRYING??"

Many people have triggers when they are asked to speak in public or give a presentation at work. It is a situation that is uncomfortable, and the stakes often feel high because failure *is* an option. Even the anticipation of talking in front of people (especially the *anticipation*), can activate the Backseat Driver's voice. Maybe it says to you, "Why would anyone care about what you have to say?" or "You are horrible at public speaking," or "What if someone asks you a question and you don't know the answer?" Do any of these voices sound familiar? Have you heard anyone say those words to you before? Triggers often cause physical reactions as well – a pit in your stomach, a flushed face, sweaty palms, or a shiver down the spine. These are the physical reactions to the hormones being released in your bloodstream. Noticing these signals helps you identify *when* you are in a state of reaction – when you are feeling triggered.

Think about this in the context of *Finding Your Z*. What if you are thinking about quitting your stable, well-paying corporate job to start a business you've been dreaming about for years? You can bet Irene will have a field day with that one, given the uncertainty and risk that inevitably comes with starting your own company. The Backseat Driver doesn't care about excitement, fulfillment, and unlimited potential for income – it wants safe, stable, and predictable. It might say things like, "Are you crazy? Why would you quit a perfectly good job for something that has no guarantee of success?" Or if your Irene is particularly crafty and mean, she might say something like, "You are being irresponsible – don't you know you have a family to support? You are going to put their lives and security in jeopardy!"

Irene needs to go jump in a lake.

“ You have been criticizing yourself for years, and it hasn't worked. Try approving of yourself and see what happens. ”

LOUISE HAY

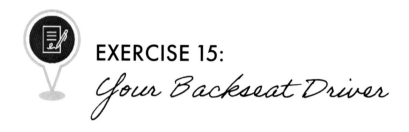

EXERCISE 15:
Your Backseat Driver

Notice when your Backseat Driver appears in your life (*notice the trigger*) and what happens in your head and body. **Take a moment to name your Backseat Driver and write down the words or phrases they use to hold you back and keep you comfortable.**

The name of my Backseat Driver is: _____

The circumstances which most frequently bring out my Backseat Driver's voice are:

_____

_____

_____

_____

When that happens, this is what my Backseat Driver says to me:

_____

_____

_____

_____

EXERCISE 16:
Your Ride or Die

Now that we have given your Backseat Driver a name, identified what activates them, and tuned into what it says to you, it is time to leave your Backseat Driver on the side of the road. If you recognize the reality of having a "little voice in your head" who whispers terrible things to you, then it is possible to create a little voice that whispers encouraging words to you, right? Let's develop an Antidote – an Inner Hero – *Your Ride or Die*. This is the voice you need sitting Shotgun in your life if you are a dream chaser. This voice will remind you to ignore crazy Irene in the backseat.

We recommend giving Your Ride or Die a name too. This time, select a name you like – one that represents strength, confidence, compassion, or pumps you up and makes you feel good. In our illustration, we use the name Grace, which represents the *grace* you need to grant yourself. Every time Irene rears her ugly head, you can say – "I see you Irene. I know you are just trying to protect me, but I'm going to need you to shut up," and then ask yourself what would *Grace* say instead?

Here's one way to adjust your soundtrack in the moment to TURN UP Grace, and TURN DOWN Irene. First, start by looking for evidence that is grounded in what is actually happening. Is there more evidence to support what Irene is saying to you or more evidence to the contrary?

Let's go back to the example of speaking in public:

- *Trigger:* You are asked to speak at an upcoming sales conference, which makes you nervous, uncomfortable, and activates a major case of the imposter syndrome.

- *Irene Says:* "You're going to sound like an idiot and people will ask you all kinds of questions you don't know the answers to, and you'll look like a fool."

- **Stop and Get Curious. Ask Yourself** – "Is that really true? Do I know what they are going to ask me? Will I be expected to know all of the answers?"

- **Look for the Evidence:** I have given speeches before, and even though it isn't my favorite thing to do, it has actually been fine. I didn't die, I didn't faint, and no one told me afterward that I sounded like an idiot. In fact, they told me I did a good job.

- **Listen to Grace:** "You've got this! You have demonstrated in the past that you are a successful speaker and people need to hear what you have to say. You are knowledgeable about the topic, you have prepared thoroughly, and you are going to absolutely crush this speech!"

See how that works? What evidence is there in your life to support Grace's voice instead of that pesky Irene? It's time to kick Irene out of your backseat and make room for Grace in the shotgun seat! Alright – it's time to name your Ride or Die, your inner hero, your Shotgun.

My Ride or Die's Name Is: _____

What could your *Ride or Die* say that would be an antidote to your Backseat Driver?

_____

_____

_____

_____

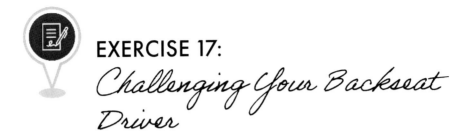

EXERCISE 17:
Challenging Your Backseat Driver

Now, let's pull it all together. This exercise might take some time but it can be a life changer! People who really dig in here will be able to routinely leave Irene by the side of the road when she pops up in the Backseat. You can't stop Irene – her voice will always be there – but you can learn to silence her so her voice takes up less and less space in your head.

 CAUTION: Skipping this part could derail your path to Z.

This exercise is organized into four columns.

- **Column #1 is for the *Triggers*.** These are the events that cause your Backseat Driver to show up, slinging insults at you. Write down the triggers you can think of – for example, when you are trying new things, speaking up in meetings, or looking in the mirror.

- **Column #2 is for the voice of your *Backseat Driver*.** What does your Backseat Driver say to you when those events happen? For every trigger, capture what your Backseat Driver says to you. What happens inside your head?

- **Column #3 is for *Evidence*.** Think about what your Backseat Driver is saying to you. Is it true? Is it based on things that have actually happened? Are they exaggerating? What evidence do you have that either confirms or refutes what your Backseat Driver is saying to you? Maybe there is a thread of truth, but it might be something that is a "growth edge" for you – meaning, you might not be an expert in it yet or are imperfect in your practice, but you are in learning mode and making thoughtful choices.

- **Column #4 is for _Your Ride or Die_.** Given the evidence presented, what could your inner hero say to you as an antidote to the limiting beliefs and inner critic in your head?

The antidote might not be the exact opposite of what your Backseat Driver says. It could be a more loving acknowledging of where you have opportunities to learn and grow. For example, let's say your trigger is that you want to quit your unfulfilling job and start your own business selling cupcakes, but you are terrified of failure.

- **_The Backseat Driver Says:_** "Cupcakes? Who is going to buy cupcakes from an accountant? Who do you think you are? You are going to fail!"

So, you take a look at the Evidence.

- **Evidence:** You are actually a rock star cupcake baker. You love to make them and everyone who eats them says they are heaven. You are constantly being told you should start selling them. While you make amazing cupcakes, the reality is that you don't have any experience running a business. You don't have a business plan and are not sure where to start.

- **_Your Ride or Die Says:_** You have a talent and passion for making cupcakes. If you want it bad enough, and are willing to put in the work, you know you can make it happen. You are an amazing accountant, and you could use those skills to help you create a business plan. You should learn more about what it takes to run your own business before taking the leap but you think you'd LOVE this career!

The antidote doesn't have to be a 100% cheerleader – it just needs to shift from inner beratement into constructive and supportive beliefs that will help you get to where you are going.

Before you complete the exercise yourself, here's another example of using this model:

Trigger	Irene Says	Evidence	Grace Says
I ate a donut when I told myself I was going to start eating healthy today.	You are weak. You can't even go one day without stuffing your face. You are disgusting and you have no willpower whatsoever. You will be fat forever. You might as well give up.	It was one donut, and for the rest of the day and week I made really healthy choices. Eating healthy is a journey for me and this was one choice of many other choices I've made.	You got this. One donut is not going to derail your progress. Make a better choice next time and move on. I know this is really important to you and you can do it!

Now it's your turn. Take your time on this exercise. Be brutally honest about what your Backseat Driver says to you even when (particularly when) it is hard to hear. Don't censor it.

Trigger	My Backseat Driver Says	Evidence	My Ride or Die Says

Here's the thing about your Backseat Driver — however and whenever they show up, it takes active, constant work to keep their voice at bay. You may not always recognize when it pops up. Even if you're super evolved and have done your inner work over months and months, you can still be susceptible to your Backseat Driver's voice. The work ahead is to continue to become aware of your common triggers, recognize what happens, call it out (*Hey Irene — I see you!*), and learn to silence it so it has less and less power over you (*Take a hike, Irene!*). Just like you do with those people who you don't want to have influence in your life anymore, put Irene in the Cheap Seats!

REFLECTING ON YOUR BACKSEAT DRIVER
Questions We Explored

1. How does your inner dialogue impact your ability to reach goals and pursue your ideal life?

2. What are the situations that activate your inner critic (aka your Backseat Driver)?

3. In those situations, what does your Backseat Driver say to you?

4. How can you manage your Backseat Driver?

Your Backseat Driver is not going away, but you can make it harder to hear them. It is your choice how close and loud you will let them be in your life. Having a full tank helps you move forward faster.

Let's get some Fuel in you!

Chapter 8:

FUELING YOUR JOURNEY

FUELING YOUR JOURNEY
Questions to Explore

- What are the resources I need to fuel my journey to Z?

- Which resources are low in my life, and how can I fill them back up?

- How does having a full fuel tank help me reach my Z?

If we're lucky, the journey of our life is long and filled with choices — numerous opportunities will present themselves and we will need to navigate through them. Building a life that is aligned to your Z is not easy — while you may have a clear vision for what you want, you will continually be challenged with obstacles, fears, other people's opinions, unexpected life events, and so on. Your journey to Z will require tenacity, stamina, perseverance, and resilience.

And all of those things require FUEL.

Our Story

When we were looking for a story that would help readers appreciate the importance of fuel in *Finding Your Z*, we realized the answer was right in front of our noses. It was us! As mentioned in the Introduction, we made the decision to write *Finding Your Z* together in 2019 after seeing how this framework helped others. We were inspired to alleviate the suffering of those who felt lost or overwhelmed by the choices they were facing in life. FUELED by the support of our families, we built a website, a social media strategy, designed a workshop, created a keynote speech, and even traveled the country shooting videos about people on their path to Z – we were racing toward an armchair on Oprah's Super Soul Sunday (*Hey Oprah! If you are reading this, that is still on our vision board! Call us!*).

Then, life happened BIG-TIME. Michelle received a big promotion at work in late 2019, which took up more of her time and energy. Candyce's business, *The People Side*, was growing rapidly and requiring more of her attention and money. We are both moms with kids who have busy, active lives and our husbands both have demanding careers as well. So we decided to slow down the pace of writing and release the book in 2020 instead. Uh, huh. I mean, who knew?

When the COVID-19 pandemic hit, 70% of Candyce's business disappeared in 2 weeks – every class was canceled, and she had to hustle just to keep the lights on. Michelle started working 60+ hours a week as she tried to keep the employees of a cereal manufacturing company healthy and safe so they could continue to produce food for America. All of the inspiration, passion, energy, momentum, and time we needed for our *Finding Your Z* project just disappeared. Like many people during the pandemic, we felt depleted by the disappointment of trips not taken, our kids learning at home, and just plain WORRYING about the health and safety of our families and loved ones. We drank too much wine, spent sleepless nights fretting about the racial injustices happening in our backyard (Minneapolis), and missed spending time with our friends and family. Eighteen months passed with little to no work on the book. We were so far from *Finding Your Z*, literally and figuratively.

Sometimes you need to rest. Sometimes it just isn't the right season of your life for dream chasing. What matters is that you notice when you feel depleted and shift gears. If your WHY is front and center, and your "Z" is important enough to reach, you will make it happen. It just requires more fuel and a new timeline.

FUELING YOUR JOURNEY

Let's talk about the "fuel" you will need on your path to Z. Think about your fuel reserves as a set of gauges with "E" representing how we feel when we are depleted and "F" representing how we feel when we are abundant or full. We will explore five types of fuels that you will need to reach your destination. As you read about each of them, consider where your gauges currently are and how they will impact you realizing your ambitions. The work of *Finding Your Z* requires you to have some amount of *Time, Money, Wellness, Support,* and *Grit* to be successful. We'll explore each of these areas to determine if you are set up for success!

TYPES OF FUEL

TIME

Oh TIME, you are a tricky little minx. We just can't get enough of you and you move on so quickly. How many times have you said to someone, "I don't have enough time to do that" or even worse, "I ran out of time and missed my chance." That one is heartbreaking. The truth is, you do have time. We all do. We all have the same 24 hours to use in the pursuit of what is important to us. What we lack is the management of that time. We don't prioritize our precious time and say *yes* to things we should say *no* to. You only need to look at your Weekly Screen Time report to see that you actually have time on your hands. To get to Z, you are going to have to become the boss of your time.

Let's say you are planning a road trip to a destination that is 300 miles away and you leave your house in the morning with a gas tank that is half-full even though there are no gas stations between you and your destination. Do you think you are going to get there? Of course not! How is it that we expect to achieve our goals in life and get to Z on a half-tank of *Time*? Your dream will take a certain amount of time to achieve – to search for jobs, to learn a new skill, to create that product, or to write that page. You need to account for it.

Said differently, imagine that the gas gauge is filled with 24 hours. Let's assume that in a typical 24-hour day, you get a solid 8 hours of sleep (more on that in a moment), spend 1 hour getting ready for your day, have a 30-minute commute to work, work an 8-hour day, and then have another 30-minute commute home. You spend 1 hour preparing meals, and another hour consuming them. If you are doing the math, that is 20 hours! That leaves you 4 precious hours to work toward whatever your Z is each day – investing in your relationships, investing in your health, investing in your future – 4 hours! What if you spend 2 of those 4 hours scrolling through social media looking at the lives of people you don't care about or don't know? What if the impact of doing that actually diminishes your energy, and leaves you feeling insecure or jealous of the highlight reels people share online? Or you spend 2 hours zoned out binge-watching your latest Netflix find? We aren't saying we don't deserve downtime. But what if you spent 2 of your 4 hours investing in your dreams instead? Again, do the math with us here. If you spent just 2 hours every day working toward your dreams, with 2 weeks off for vacation and total relaxation, that ends up being 702 hours you'll have available for dream chasing! You better believe that if you invest 702 hours in chasing your dreams this year, you won't be at the same letter next year. You get the point – you have the time. You just need a plan out your time and have the discipline to honor it in pursuit of your Z. Then once you achieve your dreams, you can post your pictures on social media for all your friends to admire because you should be very proud.

MONEY

Nobody likes to talk about money, but the reality is we all need it. You know the saying, "You have to have money to make money?" There is a reason that saying exists – because it is largely true! If your dream is to start a new business, or build your dream house, or take your family to Disney World, that is going to require money – which will require you managing it. Not unlike time, if we really look closely at our money and our expenses, many people would be appalled at their leaky gas tanks. Five dollars for coffee here, $50 for a manicure there, $100 to eat out because we don't feel like cooking – it all adds up. Where we spend our money is a direct reflection of our priorities. For example, Candyce's family spends an extraordinary amount of money on traveling the world together because they decided that was one of their priorities. They set aside cash every year to make that happen. You can create a budget for what matters to you, but a leaky gas tank can leave you stranded alongside the road about 50 miles short of your goals if you aren't careful. Creating a plan for your money is just as important as planning how you are going to spend your time. We don't know about you, but the word "BUDGET" feels heavy and restrictive. It sounds like a chore. What if you called it your "FREEDOM PLAN" or your "Z ACCOUNT?" That sounds like something worth putting your money into, doesn't it? In addition to controlling your spending – where your money goes – you might also need to generate more fuel by picking up a side gig, putting in extra hours at your current job, or even selling things you no longer use. There are many ways to start funding your journey to Z; it just requires planning and intention.

WELLNESS

To what degree does your current health and well-being support your journey to Z? Do you neglect things like exercise or a healthy diet because you don't have the time or energy to put into it? It is hard to get to Z in a broken-down jalopy. To have the stamina to overcome the bumps and potholes of life, your body (*your vehicle*) needs to be finely tuned and in tip-top shape. What are some things you can do to ensure that you have the energy to achieve your dreams?

- **EAT:** Most of us realize that our diet significantly impacts our energy. Do you prioritize eating nutritious, whole foods that make your body feel good? Which foods give you a lift, and which ones make you want to take a nap? Do you plan meals in advance or prepare food ahead of time? The work of getting to your Z is time consuming, so if you plan ahead, you are less likely to find your hand in a bag chips or running through a drive-thru out of pure convenience. That kind of behavior won't fuel your Z.

- **MOVE:** How about exercise? Do you schedule movement into your day? Even a 30-minute walk, or a quick stretch break, can get your heart pumping and your body moving in a way that primes you for the work that lies ahead. Not to mention, that some of the best ideas can come from a head-clearing walk or spending time in the great outdoors. So go do something you enjoy – something that requires you to move your body!

- **SLEEP:** Along with a healthy diet and moving your body, getting adequate sleep is a habit that ensures your machine is running smoothly. For most adults, at least 7 hours of sleep a night is required to keep all of your systems working as they should. How do you prepare for a good night of sleep? Consider limiting the use of electronics for at least an hour before bed, keep your bedroom as cool and dark as possible, and limit your intake of caffeine, large meals, and alcohol late in the day to set yourself up for a great night of rest.

- **MENTAL HEALTH:** Practicing meditation, writing in a journal, utilizing aromatherapy, doing yoga, breathing deeply, or going to therapy are all practices that are proven to alleviate anxiety and stress. Find what works for you! Speaking to a trusted friend or therapist about your dreams and the stress you feel can be helpful, too. Additionally, surround yourself with positive, supportive people who help you see what's possible instead of pointing out what could go wrong.

SUPPORT

We've already discussed the importance of WHO is in your life, and how their voices impact you, but do you know when to pull those people in and ask for their help and support? What good is it to have supportive people around you if you don't tell them when you need their help? You are not on this journey alone. It is rare for someone to get to Z without the help and support of a community with open ears and helping hands. It is not a sign of weakness to ask for help – instead, it is a sign that you are serious about realizing your ideal life. As we discussed in the *Finding Your WHO* section, if you don't have the right people in your Band to provide support - go look for them. Find people who have done what you are trying to do and tap into their knowledge and expertise. Find a community of people who understand what it takes to reach Z because they are already on their own paths. When we wanted to write a book, we talked to others who had written books asking for their advice (*Thanks Steph and Greg!*), and when we ran out of gas we talked to our husbands and friends who encouraged us to start back up again. Our husbands sent us away for weeks to write while they held down the fort at home (*Thanks Fred & Brent!*) and our teams at work covered for us (*Thanks Team!*). But our biggest cheerleaders were our daughters who wore *Finding Your Z* T-shirts, ordered laptop stickers with our logo on them, and presold books to their friends all before we had a first draft! Without their encouragement and support, we honestly would not have been able to cross the finish line.

GRIT

You will need some resilience to get through the inevitable twists, turns, and roadblocks that stand between you and your Z. Our friends Brent and Dani – who developed an awesome wellness program for companies called *LeadWell* – call this characteristic "Bounce"

Having grit is the same thing as having BOUNCE: the ability to get knocked down but get up again and move forward.

Some people also call this ability to bounce back *Grit*. Grit is the "stick-to-it-ness" some people have when life gets hard. Do you know anyone who will throw up their hands and give up at the slightest sign of tension? Do you also know people who see obstacles as just another "interesting challenge" or "tricky problem" to solve? If you tend to stall out and get stuck in a state of wallowing when bad things happen – hosting a two-month pity party for yourself because the condo you wanted sold before you signed the lease – that might be the real obstacle you need to overcome. People with grit jump right over that hurdle and start looking for another condo. Grit is a mind-set. The degree to which you are able to anticipate, process, and even welcome setbacks is a measure of your grit.

Here's an example of how two different people in the same situation, with different levels of grit, managed through detours that occurred while building their dreams:

> Melissa and Shawnda are opening up a franchise of the same makeup company. The supplier informs them that the new product for the spring line, which they are counting on to launch their business in a big way, has been delayed for two months.
>
> While both are frustrated and disappointed, Melissa completely becomes paralyzed and feels victimized. She might think things like, "That stupid supplier is going to ruin the launch of my business. There is nothing I can do but wait for this product to show up. I was counting on them and they failed me." She might even decide that she isn't going to open her business at all because she now feels spooked by the unpredictable nature of working with suppliers.
>
> Shawnda, by contrast, starts thinking about all of the ways she can build anticipation into her future customer base – she sees these additional two months as a gift that will actually allow her the time she needs to develop an amazing marketing campaign, which will make her business launch even better! She sees this "disaster" as an opportunity.
>
> The mindset shift Shawnda has when faced with obstacles makes her better positioned to get to Z. When there is a boulder in the middle of her path, she doesn't just sit in her car waiting for a big crane to

come and move the boulder out of her way, she does a U-turn and finds another route to her destination. That's grit. And the harder your life has been up to this point, the more grit you probably have. Believing you have the personal "mastery" to control your mindset and your response to adversity, the more resilient you will be. The more you use the word "yet" the more grit you have. If you are not good at something, you are not good at something YET. That's a growth mindset, and you are going to need it!

66 Be patient with yourself. Self-growth is tender; it's holy ground. There's no greater investment. **99**

STEPHEN COVEY

EXERCISE 18:

How Much Fuel is In Your Tank?

I n the following exercise, we will have you consider each of the five fuel sources — Time, Money, Wellbeing, Support, and Grit — and provide a description of a "Full Tank." How would you mark your fuel gauge by comparison? Indicate on the gauge where you think you are in response to each of these statements using the range of "Empty" to "Full."

> **TIME** – I have enough time in my day to focus on the things that matter to me. I routinely say "no" to the things that sabotage my happiness, and intentionally invest my precious time in the things I want to say "yes" to. My schedule is aligned with my priorities in life.

What is preventing you from having a full "TIME" tank?

_____

_____

_____

MONEY – I have enough money to enjoy my life. I intentionally manage my finances to ensure my investments are aligned with my priorities. I am able to reach my goals financially and have a healthy relationship with spending.

What is preventing you from having a full "MONEY" tank?

_____

_____

_____

WELLNESS – I invest the necessary amount of time required to stay in good physical and mental health. I feel good about my nutrition, exercise, and sleep habits. I have appropriate outlets for managing my stress and recognize the importance of self-care.

What is preventing you from having a full "WELLNESS" tank?

_____

_____

SUPPORT – I have people in my life who support my dreams and I ask for their assistance when needed. I routinely build my network and seek out the people I need to know in order to achieve my life goals.

What is preventing you from having a full "SUPPORT" tank?

_____

_____

_____

GRIT – I expect to run into obstacles and challenges in my life. I am not easily deterred or distracted by these setbacks. I view obstacles as opportunities for exploring new paths. I do not ruminate on how I wish things would be, but instead I control what I can.

What is preventing you from having a full "GRIT" tank?

_____

_____

_____

If you marked FULL on each of these gauges, congratulations! You are a superhero! For the majority of us, there will be areas that are fuller than others, and there will be gauges that are downright EMPTY. That's okay! If you're on EMPTY on any of these gauges, it doesn't mean you cannot start to pursue or reach your Z. It just means that you would find it valuable to create some capacity or take new actions that would fill yourself up with these things. All of them are available to you, if only you choose to make them a priority. Imagine what it will feel like to reach those Bold Goals you set, or live in your Happy Place? It is worth it to fuel your journey so you can get there faster?

EXERCISE 19:
Fill Your Tank

Let's take a few minutes to explore each of these areas and talk about some ways that you can make your tanks a little fuller! What is your plan for *fueling* your journey to Z? What are 1 to 2 things that you want to START or STOP doing to fill your tank more in each of these areas?

TIME

1. _____
_____
_____

2. _____
_____
_____

MONEY

1. _____
_____
_____

2. _____
_____
_____

WELLNESS

1. _____
_____
_____

2. _____
_____
_____

SUPPORT

1. _____
   _____
   _____
   _____

2. _____
   _____
   _____
   _____

GRIT

1. _____
   _____
   _____
   _____

2. _____
   _____
   _____
   _____

REFLECTING ON FUELING YOUR JOURNEY
Questions We Explored

- What are the resources I need to fuel my journey to Z?

- Which resources are low in my life, and how can I fill them back up?

- How would a fuller fuel tank help me reach my Z?

Through these exercises and your personal reflections, we hope you recognize the importance of FUEL so that you don't run out of gas before you get to your Z. We hope that by putting an action plan together you will have the right amount of TIME, MONEY, WELLNESS, SUPPORT, and GRIT to continue driving in the direction of your dreams.

Now, let's hear from people who can attest to the need for fuel on the road to Z. They have already encountered some of the obstacles you will face.

Let's call this next part "STORIES FROM THE ROAD."

Chapter 9:

STORIES FROM THE ROAD

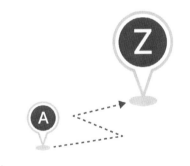

STORIES FROM THE ROAD
Questions to Explore

- What "trade-offs" will you confront on your journey to Z?

- How will you react to the unexpected but inevitable obstacles you face?

Kent's Story

Kent's family owned a used car/truck dealership in the small town where he grew up. It had been in his family since his grandfather started the company in the 1920s. Kent worked in the family business, along with his dad and brother, from the time he left high school until his late 40s. Around that time, his dad decided to retire, and shortly thereafter, Kent's brother suffered a seizure at work. Unfortunately, the seizure ended up being the symptom of a brain tumor and cancer that had spread to the rest of his brother's body. After a long, hard battle, his brother lost his fight with cancer. What was once a family business was now a business run by a single family member, Kent, which was not feasible. There were no other sons, daughters, or cousins interested in continuing the business, so Kent found himself at a crossroads wondering what to do. He could hire employees to keep the business running or use this as an opportunity to pursue other interests and dreams he'd had earlier in his life. So at the age of 48, Kent decided to go back to college to earn an education in drafting. It required a lot of work, learning things he had never done before – including the proper way to double-click a mouse! After college, he secured a job as a drafter with a steel fabrication company where he happily worked until his retirement. While there was no way to predict the events that led to this life-changing decision, Kent recognized that sometimes it takes an extraordinary event to push us into extraordinary action. While the circumstances that created the detour were sad and tragic, they resulted in an opportunity for him to reflect and reinvent his life.

“ Do not judge me by my success, judge me by how many times I fell down and got back up again. ”

NELSON MANDELA

STORIES FROM
THE ROAD

I nevitably, on your journey to Z, you will encounter situations, people, and insecurities that get in your way. Roadblocks are a reality of life and have the capacity
to stall you out and stop your progress. The key is to expect they *will* happen – in
fact, encountering obstacles and challenges on your journey to Z is a near certainty.
And not unlike real roadblocks, all you will control is your reaction to them.

Life happens, no matter how much planning, budgeting, and striving you do. Life likes
to derail our best laid plans. We need to be open to the unexpected bumps in the
road because they can send us in a totally different and potentially even more positive
direction – we have all heard stories that involve bad things becoming the best thing
that ever happened to someone. Remember Andy's story in *Finding Your WHY?* You
can bet that Andy and his family didn't view Stage 4 cancer as a gift when they heard
those words from the oncologist. It took an enormous amount of courage, reflection,
grief, anger, bargaining, heartache, and ultimately love to get Andy and his family to
realize that cancer had something to teach them. As a result, they made some serious
U-turns in their life that ended up being extremely positive for their family. How you
choose to respond is the only control you have in a moment like that.

The journey to Z takes time – in fact, it takes a lifetime. The people around you are
going to change, the circumstances around you are going to change, and the world
is going to change. If there is anything the last decade has taught us, it's that life as
we know it can be disrupted in an instant. You can choose to see that disruption as
devastating and allow it to derail your progress toward Z or you can view it as an

exit ramp – a chance to recalculate your route and head in a different, but equally fulfilling direction.

One of the most common roadblocks people experience with *Finding Your Z* is making decisions about one component of their life without taking into account the other elements. For example, how often do you compartmentalize your work life from your personal life? When you separate the two and look at them as different parts of yourself rather than interrelated parts of your life, you are at risk for making poor career decisions. This is not to say that all work/career decisions will negatively affect your WHO, WHY, and WHERE, but the important thing is to be aware of *how* they will be impacted and make a conscious, intentional choice with that awareness. It might require having hard conversations with people in your life. As we've said previously, because it is based on the alphabet, using the *Finding Your Z* framework is a way you can have a conversation with your loved ones using a common language.

For example, if you describe your dream life as you understand it now (your "Z") and share that you currently feel like you are at the letter "F" that provides a lot of context for them. Now, imagine that you are wanting move forward in your alphabet and say "YES!" to an opportunity that feels like the letter "M" for you. Seeing how far that moves you towards "Z" may explain why you are willing to make some tradeoffs and try it out.

The *Finding Your Z* framework also allows people to share their own "Z" with you and explain how the decision you are contemplating may affect them. Realizing the trade-offs you are asking them to make is important data for you to have in your decision making! Maybe they feel like they are at the letter "R" but your decision impacts them negatively, and they sense it would take them back to the letter "G" for example. You can see how this framework may makes things clearer, but these conversations will never be easy.

Your loved ones have their own WHY, WHO, WHAT, and WHERE that will require collaborative conversations about trade-offs. For example, you may decide that your dream job is one where you'll be traveling away from home 80% of the time. If your loved ones need your help or care, you can bet that you being gone 80% of the time is not going to work well for them. Your decision requires some serious conversations and creative problem-solving. It doesn't mean it can't happen or that it's off the table, it just means you need to get the people involved together to problem-solve so it doesn't strain or destroy your relationship. It may mean hiring a housecleaner or a nanny, or finding other solutions that support the needs of your family. Maybe the job can be negotiated down to 50% travel instead of 80%, and still be your dream job? These are all creative considerations that allow people to continue to chase their dreams.

One way to approach these decisions is to acknowledge and document the trade-offs each of you are making and evaluate them one by one. Get real about what you are signing up for and being asked to give up on. Consider if those trade-offs are worth it. That is the value of integrating your WHY, WHO, WHERE, and WHAT so you have a whole life approach.

The following story could have prevented. It is an example of someone who wishes she would have had a well thought out "trade-off" conversation with her family instead of a conversation that ended up changing everything.

Heather's Story

Heather was approached about a job opportunity in London and was thrilled to tell her family that they would be moving there with her for a three-year assignment. When she came home and spilled this news at the dinner table, eyes brimming with excitement and possibility, her husband was shocked into silence. He owned his own business and they had just built their new house two years earlier. Moving to London seemed crazy and he was immediately upset that she would even consider it. They ended up fighting that night, and many nights afterward, resulting in Heather turning down the London job and taking a new part-time job as someone "Fostering Resentment." Resentment which ultimately destroyed her marriage within a year.

Fast forward 18 months and Heather happens to be sitting in a leadership development program with Candyce. When she hears about the *Finding Your Z* concept, she becomes visibly emotional.

Heather and Candyce talked after class and she explained that she wished she'd known about *Finding Your Z* the day she received the offer to go to London. Heather shared, "If I had sat my family down and explained that I felt like I was at the letter 'D' in my life and that the London job would leapfrog me to like a 'S' I think my husband would have listened. But I couldn't articulate any of that in a way he could appreciate. And he was unable to help me understand why he wouldn't consider going. From my point of view, I felt that our family made a lot of trade-offs to get his business off of the ground so he was way closer to his Z than I was to mine. I had kept the steady job with steady benefits and now I was further behind in terms of my fulfillment, flexibility, and happiness. To me, moving to London would be his turn to pay me back! I could not forgive him for not seeing my side and my family fell apart because of it. I'm 44 years old and back to the beginning of the alphabet. There isn't a job out there that can get me to Z now. My family, my house, and the life we shared were a huge part of my Z, which I ruined because I was only thinking about my career." It was heartbreaking, and also sadly familiar. To say that we have coached hundreds of leaders in their second or third marriages due to poor career calls is not an over exaggeration!

Heather's story may be relatable to you. We don't live our lives alone. The decisions we make impact other people. Neither Heather nor her husband could reach their Z without the other person's support. Our ability to communicate with others where we are at and what we want is critical when facing big life decisions. *Finding Your Z* isn't just about finding the life we want, it is also about helping others in your life find their Z, too. This framework has enabled countless people to navigate the life-changing conversations that need to happen between couples, families, parents, coaches, managers, and friends during this thing called life.

There is a small silver lining in Heather's story and what she took away from *Finding Your Z* that day. During their conversation, Candyce asked if sharing these insights would help her move forward with her ex-husband even though they weren't together. She thought it was worth a shot. Although they did not magically reunite after their *Finding Your Z* talk (wouldn't THAT have been a great story!), Heather told Candyce that she felt like they finally listened to each other and felt understood – a huge step forward! This shared language and understanding improved their communication as parents and friends.

Next we will talk about *Detours and U-Turns*, which can often be necessary on your path to Z, when things happen to or around you that are beyond your control. They aren't always unhappy events, either. Sometimes unexpected positive things can send you off in a different direction. Other times, unhappy things can later end up being the best thing that could have ever happened to you.

We can be at a point in our lives where things are really, really good – we are moving and grooving, sailing through the alphabet on our way to Z, and we think – it just can't get any better than this, I am crushing this Z thing! Then life happens. No one can predict events like economic recessions (unless you're a trained economist) or global pandemics (unless you're a trained epidemiologist) or predict exactly how our lives will be impacted. What really matters is your mindset about the change. You can choose to see a particular change or event as devastating and allow it to strand you alongside the road, completely derailing your progress toward your Z, or you can instead see it as simply an exit ramp or detour – taking you in a different, unexpected but equally (or potentially more) fulfilling direction.

There is a psychological concept called "post-traumatic growth," which essentially refers to the growth or positive transformation people experience following a traumatic event. Developed by psychologists Richard Tedeschi, PhD and Lawrence Calhoun, PhD, in the mid-1990s, the theory is that post-trauma, some experience a new awareness of their inner strength, resilience, capability, or appreciation for life. The trauma might cause people to look at the world or their circumstances through a different lens, potentially revealing a renewed or different purpose in life – a higher calling. We call this a clearer understanding of our realignment of your WHY. "People develop new understandings of themselves, the world they live in, how to relate to other people, the kind of future they might have and a better understanding of how to live life," says Tedeschi. Tedeschi and Calhoun even created a scale called the Post Traumatic Growth Inventory, which measures people's positive responses after experiencing trauma in the following areas: appreciation of life, relationships with others, and new possibilities in life, personal strength and spiritual change (*Journal of Traumatic Stress*, 1996).

Along with experiencing hard times or working through something with a series of setbacks comes an opportunity to learn, grow, and build resilience. Resilience is the capability to pick yourself up and dust yourself off after being knocked down – and how well you bounce back from disappointment, mistakes, failure, or difficult circumstances. Resilience is the key to *Finding Your Z*. We guarantee that the bigger the leap you try to make toward your Z, the harder you'll be knocked down. You might find yourself in a ten-car pileup with traffic at a dead stop on your road to Z. It might require you to do a U-turn and take an exit 5 letters back. You might have to go back to your internal GPS and figure out a different route to get where you want to go. The stakes become higher the further you get into your journey and the setbacks can be even more painful. When you get knocked back by life, your resilience will determine how long you stay there. This doesn't mean you can't be sad or angry or disappointed, or any other normal human emotions. You get to spend time doing that. Feel the feelings and move forward anyway. The people who reach their Z get back on the road, and only glance in the rearview mirror. They move on.

❝ She stood in the storm, and when the wind did not blow her way, she adjusted her sails. **❞**

ELIZABETH EDWARDS

EXERCISE 20:
Building Resilience

Take a moment to reflect upon the most difficult experience you have faced in your life. What did you learn about yourself during that situation? How did it shift your worldview? Did you develop new strengths or capabilities? How did you use that experience as an opportunity (or even an accelerator) on your path to Z?

Viewing obstacles as learning experiences will impact your ability to be resilient and reach your Z. Don't hold onto your vision of Z too tightly – let it evolve as you evolve. As changes occur, you may learn something new about yourself or gain clarity on what is really important to you. Z is not intended to be viewed as the end of your life or retirement, it is meant to be a compass for living your ideal life, as you know it to be today. It should not be viewed as a final destination, rather it is pointing you in the general direction of a life you envision, based on your assessment and continual reassessment of your WHY, WHO, WHERE, and WHAT.

Every experience we have in life has the possibility to change any one of the components of your Z. What if you are single and get married, or are childless and become a parent, or are married and get a divorce? Those changes tend to cause a significant shift in our worldview, and a recalculation of our ideal life. Reflect back on the story of Jonathan, who despite being 26 years old, felt like he had reached his Z. He had his hot girlfriend, a great job, great friends, and was making more money than he ever had before – but what feels important to you at 26 can looks very different at 46, and will look different again at 66. Your life experiences twist the lenses of your self-awareness over time to help you gain more and more clarity about who you are and what you want. The key is to keep recalibrating when things happen. Is this a shift to your Z or a total overhaul? Are you going to keep moving forward, or are you going to pull over and start over? Getting to Z is the adventure of your lifetime. You will learn a lot as you go.

REFLECTING ON STORIES FROM THE ROAD
Questions We Explored

- What "trade-offs" will you confront on your journey to Z?
- How will you react to the unexpected but inevitable obstacles you face?

If Dream Chasing was easy, we'd all be living the life of our dreams right now. The most successful people are those who anticipate hardship and challenge because they are not derailed when it happens. In fact, the more challenging your life has been, the more prepared you are for chasing your dreams. The struggle has made you stronger and it has taught you how to respond to life's detours and U-turns. Your past prepared you for your future.

You are ready to Get in The Driver's Seat!

Chapter 10:

GET IN THE DRIVER'S SEAT

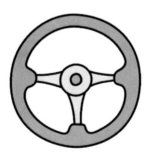

GET IN THE DRIVER'S SEAT
Questions to Explore

- How do you translate your ambitions into action?

- WHO needs to know about what you learned in this book?

- WHAT is your plan for taking the next step in your alphabet?

- WHY will you hold yourself accountable for taking this action?

Greg's Story

When we started writing this book, we talked to numerous people about their dreams and life experiences in order to make these concepts come to life. One of the people we reached out to is Greg. Candyce and Greg are friends, but she never asked him about his Z, or where he thought he was at in the alphabet until now.

Greg is a very wealthy individual – in fact he no longer has to work. He can live where he wants to live, and he can do whatever he wants to do. Greg views this freedom as an invitation to be even more clear and purposeful about how he spends his time, money, and energy. In fact, he may be the *most* intentional person we talked to during our writing process! For example, he allocates his time based upon a pie chart showing how much time he wants to spend with different people in his life – his WHO drives his schedule. Candyce passed the pie chart test and spent an entire afternoon with him discussing the concepts of our book and learning how he is purposefully creating his ideal life.

Greg was in a time of transition when she talked to him – he'd just sold the company he founded and was searching for what would be next in his life. In many ways, he was in the process of creating a new alphabet for himself. Greg thinks about life in terms of seasons – when you are a child you are in the spring of your life, and then you enjoy the sweet summer of youth, the maturity of autumn, and finally, the winter. He felt that he was still in the early autumn of his life, with plenty of energy and ambition left in the tank. He wanted an extraordinary life, and had all of the necessary fuel to realize it.

Greg reads over 300 books a year. Read that again…300 BOOKS! One book he read suggested there would be value in creating Personal Values, Goals, and a Mission Statement for his life – something we will help YOU do later in this chapter. Greg thoughtfully selected every word, calibrating carefully with his wife Brooke along the way, so they could realize an extraordinary and fulfilling life together. Creating this shared language has proven to be critical in their world of extreme abundance

– having a shared vision and Mission Statement provides clarity for their life choices, and helps them not waste their time or money on things that are not important to them.

Completing these exercises was incredibly revealing. Greg realized he was not done competing and winning yet – he still craved those feelings in his life. Both Greg and Brooke agreed that they wanted to stay "healthy and wealthy" and decided to hold themselves accountable for moving both of those needles in the right direction in the years to come. Greg also sensed that there was at least one more company he wanted to build in his lifetime. Greg is masterful at marketing and scaling up businesses – his books, podcasts, articles, and videos have inspired thousands of sales and marketing leaders across the world. But now he wanted to get into the ear of the entrepreneur. Specifically, he wanted to help people leading professional service firms grow, scale, and sell their businesses when the time was right. He started a company called Collective 54 and intentionally did not take the CEO position. Instead, he wanted to be the Chief Investment Officer – a role that allowed him to provide advice, intellectual property, and funding to entrepreneurs. He knew that this role would provide him more flexibility and fulfillment than running the company on a daily basis and it was more in alignment with his values. Living with full integrity and self-awareness proved to be powerful. Collective 54 is on pace to be the most successful company Greg has owned so far – in fact, what he thought was his finish line, proved to just be a stepping stone.

If you've ever wondered what successful people do to become and stay successful, that is what we are teaching you to do. Not only are we providing you with the framework and tools, we are helping you use the alphabet to calibrate your progress over the future months and years of your life. Greg invests significant time and energy into realizing his ideal life – in fact, every 90 days he revisits his goals, values, and mission to ensure he is still living life in alignment with his intentions. His Mission Statement is engraved on a metal card that he carries around to hold himself accountable. It sits right next to his credit cards as a literal gut-check before he spends money. In many ways, Greg is an example of someone who is completely in the Driver's Seat of his life, and he is barreling toward his definition of Z every day. The exercises included in this chapter will help YOU do the same.

GET IN THE DRIVER'S SEAT

You now have the roadmap and keys to *Finding Your Z*. Knowing what you want is the starting line. There are 26 letters in the alphabet and you are somewhere along that path already. By now, you should have a pretty good idea of your WHY, your WHO, your WHERE, and your WHAT. Your Z is more clearly on the horizon – but how are you going to get there? This is where the proverbial rubber meets the road! None of what we have covered so far matters if you don't DO SOMETHING about it! It's time to get in the Driver's Seat! Take yourself out of Park, or Neutral, and step on the gas! You get the idea …

What does your next leap look like, or just your next letter? What will accelerate you toward your goals? Who can help you? You can start making decisions every day to get more of what you want in life and let go of what you don't.

 With this new level of self-awareness, you should be able to:

- Allow certain professional doors to close – and lean further into your sweet spot
- Ask people to enter or leave your life
- Confidently say "Yes" or "No" when opportunities present themselves
- Spend more time in your happy places
- Clearly articulate **WHAT** you want in your life

EXERCISE 21:
Start Your Engine

We challenge you to do something right away – *in the next 24 hours* – that will get you closer to your Z. Don't waste this moment of inspiration! We know you're feeling pumped from reading this book and doing these exercises (at least, we hope you are!). Now pick something you can do immediately – heck, stop reading and go do it now – we'll wait. Apply for that job, call your mom, book that vacation, or sign up for that class. Prove to yourself that it only takes a little bit of effort to make progress.

If you recall, you completed a similar exercise at the beginning of this book. Now that you know a bit more about *Finding Your Z*, let's use the alphabet a different way.

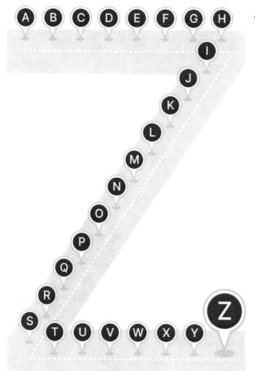

Circle the letter that you feel best represents your current location in the alphabet.

What is one *immediate* action you want to take that will get you closer to **Z** – even by one letter?

_____

COMMIT: I'm going to commit to _____ **by** _____ **(Date)**

In order to hold myself accountable, I'm going to tell _____ what I'm planning to do and by when.

Let's talk about accountability. You will be 100% more successful on your path to Z if you create accountability structures – this means you create deliberate strategies that encourage you to *do* what you say you want to do. You might need to break old habits and patterns, which involves literally rewiring your brain. (Read *Atomic Habits* by James Clear for tips on how to do this – great book!) Telling people in your life what you are doing and how they can support you is critical. If you have ever gone on a diet, you know that sitting down to a meal and telling your girlfriends you "are not eating carbs right now," will help you stay on track and not order the pasta dish or indulge in the tiramisu.

If you are wondering how to best share what you have learned about yourself from reading this book and doing the exercises, we've got you! *(Ahem … if you just read the book and didn't complete the exercises, you should go do that first. These next tools require those inputs).*

Let's create a structured way to share your insights with friends, family, and colleagues – letting them understand what you want in your life and how they can help you on your path to Z.

EXERCISE 22:
Your Mission Statement

We want to help you sum up everything you've learned about yourself into a clear and compelling Mission Statement. You can use this Mission Statement to tell people what you've realized by reading *Finding Your Z* so they can support you in an intentional way. This is a multi-step process, but by the end of it you will be able to articulate your mission in life using 15-words or less!

Reflect on what you have learned about yourself throughout this book. Complete these series of statements to help you summarize what you learned and your mission in life.

STEP 1: I learned that the most important things in my life are...
(Explain your Values – this exercise can be found in the Finding Your WHY chapter)

STEP 2: Which is why I want to spend more of my time...
(Think about your professional "Sweet Spots"– the Career Inventory exercise can be found in the Finding Your WHAT chapter. You may also reflect on your WHERE and think about the lifestyle you want).

STEP 3: I would describe "My Ideal Life" (or my "Z") as ...

(Synthesize the WHO, WHAT and WHERE exercises into a few keys phrases)

STEP 4: And right now, I feel like I am at the Letter _____. Which is why I have decided to...

(Share your intentions for reaching your Z and realizing your ideal life)

Great Work! But that would be a very long speech to make. Let's try to get all of this language boiled down into a statement that only has 15 words or less!

To do this, each word should be thoughtfully and intentionally chosen. You may go through many versions of this statement until you land on the right one. You will know you have nailed it when you say, "Wow, that's it. If I spend my entire life doing that, I will be happy and it will matter to me." When Greg wrote his Personal Mission Statement, *"To live a fulfilling life by taking risks and competing for extraordinary accomplishments,"* it hit upon a few core tenants that mattered to him — the emotion he wanted to feel (*fulfillment*) and his core values. The addition of the word "extraordinary" happened in 2019 after he sold the company he created. He and his wife Brooke had taken a trip to Cancun every year for nearly a decade, but now they were ready for new adventures, and they wanted those adventures to feel "extraordinary." This resulted in raising their vacation bar and selecting more exotic destinations — their next trips were to Japan, Italy, and Africa. The selection of the words in your Personal Mission Statement matter because they will manifest themselves as new decisions and choices. Your Mission Statement should provide clarity when you are presented with options and need to make the right choice for you. Here are a few more examples:

- **Candyce's Mission Statement:** *Creating experiences that deepen personal connections and positively impact people's lives.*
- **Michelle's Mission Statement:** *Empowering people to become who they want to be through authentic and meaningful connections.*

OK, it's your turn. Using 15 words or less, write down your Mission Statement:

Knowing what you want doesn't guarantee you will get it. People often need to rely on their network's influence or support to realize their dreams. There are a number of ways to create accountability structures in your life and enroll others in your plans. We are including a couple of optional exercises to help you get started. In the first exercise, you will invite people to share their impression of you through a "MIRROR CHECK" experience and then you will enlist people's support by "SHARING YOUR Z."

EXERCISE 23:
The Mirror Check

Have you ever wondered what people say about you when you are not around? What they really think about you, instead of the stories you might be making up in your head? For many people, the thought of overhearing other people discussing them causes discomfort and enflames their insecurities. The truth is, what people think about you matters, somewhat, if it influences your future.

One of our coaching clients didn't apply for a job because she was SURE that her boss didn't think she was qualified (when he was actually hoping she would apply and was surprised when she didn't).

Another person thought his best friends were all in great marriages so he was unwilling to share his own insecurities about his marriage because he believed they wouldn't be able to relate to him (his friends were actually relieved when he finally opened-up because they could tell he was unhappy).

We all have a reputation that precedes us, and an impression we leave behind. However, very few of us know what it is, or how to change it. In this next exercise, we suggest you determine what you want your reputation to be and then check-in with people to see how close are far off you are with the impression you want leave. Companies use this same mindset when they create advertising campaigns or encourage leaders to manage their Personal Brands. People develop an opinion of YOUR brand within moments of interacting with it. As a company, or as an individual, you can elevate or diminish someone's first impression of you with every proceeding interaction.

Your brand is the sum of your:

- **Personal Presence:** This is your physical image (appearance, body, clothing, posture), language (tone, choice of words, manners), and your interpersonal skills.

- **Personal Competence:** This is how you demonstrate your knowledge, skills, and strengths to others.

- **Personal Choices:** These are the decisions you make personally and professionally that reflect your values and discernment. From social media, to team meetings, people watch to see if your actions and intentions can be trusted.

What do you want your personal brand to be? Let's explore that!

STEP 1: MY PERSONAL BRAND (DESIRED)

People pay attention to how you present yourself. Write down the 3 to 5 words that you want people to consistently use when they describe your Personal Brand:

1. _____
2. _____
3. _____
4. _____
5. _____

STEP 2: BRAND CHECK!

Now send a text message to 10 or more people in your life asking them to send you the 3 words they use most often to describe you to others. This is the "Mirror Check" moment to see if the way you see yourself is also how others see you. Below is a sample message to help you complete this part of the exercise:

SAMPLE TEXT MESSAGE:

Hello _____ ! I'm working on some big goals this year and I could really use your honest feedback. I have intentionally selected you to do this because you are an important person in my life and I value your opinion. I know you will tell me the truth. I would like you to text me back the 3 words you most often use when describing me to someone else. I appreciate your thoughtful response because it will help me grow!

Type the message above (or something similar) into the body of text.

1. Type the message to one person in your life

2. Decide who you are sending Message #1 to

3. "Copy" the message before you send it

4. Hit "Send" on Message #1

5. Now "Paste" and send the same message to 9+ additional people. Do not use a group text! We encourage you to send this message to your immediate family (all of them – children, spouse, parents, siblings), Your Band, Your Fans, key co-workers, managers, friends, etc.

6. Then wait with bated breath for their replies …

Some of us have very funny friends. Don't be surprised if some responses make you double-over with laughter. If this happens, enjoy the joke but text back and ask them to answer again, with a more thoughtful response. You may also receive such heartfelt replies that they make you cry. And you might receive some feedback that stings a little. This is a vulnerable reality check, which provides an abundance of self-awareness, AND opens doors to a bigger conversation.

Capture All of the Words People Texted Back Describing Your Brand:

NAME	WORD ONE	WORD TWO	WORD THREE

STEP 3: REFLECTION

Reflect on the themes and differences you see in the chart above. How aligned are these words with the brand you want to have?

- **How many times did people send back the same words as your DESIRED PERSONAL BRAND?** *(The higher that number is, the more "on brand" your behavior is)*

  _____

- **Do any of the words make you CRINGE or CURIOUS?**

  _____

- **What actions do you want to take after this exercise?**

  _____

  _____

Use this reflection space below to capture your thoughts and learnings from the Mirror Check:

_____

_____

_____

How does this exercise invite me to change or adjust your behavior to be more successful in life?

_____

_____

_____

EXERCISE 24:
Sharing Your Z

Once you're clear about what you want, you can share the vision of your Z with other people. The more you share it, the more accountability you will generate – and the more likely it is that you will take action to make it happen! One of the advantages of the *Finding Your Z* concept is the ability to share your Z quickly and simply with others so they understand where you are at in the context of an alphabet. Sharing the concept helps engage others in the conversation.

To help you talk about your Z, we offer a suggested flow for the conversation. You can certainly adjust this to suit your audience or your situation, but it highlights some core elements you can include and be prepared to share:

- **Have you ever thought about your life as an alphabet? If Z was your ideal life, what letter would you be at right now?** (*Ask them to pick a letter*)

- **Why did you pick that letter?**

- **Do you know what Z is for you?**

- **I didn't either. But I recently spent time trying to figure it out and realized that my mission in life is:** (*Your Mission Statement*)

- **Right now I feel like I am at the Letter: _____**

- **To realize the life I want, I plan to:**

- **(*What are the Bold Goals, specific dreams, or next steps you want to share with them?*)**

- **When I accomplish that, I will feel like I am at the Letter _____.**

- **I would really appreciate your support and encouragement as I realize this dream. You are an important person in my life and I need your help. (*Describe how this person can support your desired professional or personal goals. How can this person hold you accountable?*)**

Any action that gets you closer to Z is an action worth taking. It doesn't have to be big, sweeping things like quitting your job, ending your marriage, selling your house, and so on. It *can* be those things, but it could be a micro-action that gets you just a little closer. Maybe it's setting up a savings account and automatically depositing a specific amount of your paycheck until you can more confidently quit your job. Maybe it's attending a networking session or updating your resume. As long as it is a forward-thinking action that feels meaningful, and your eye is on Z, that is progress! Commit, then tell people about it.

Once you do what you said you were going to do, it's time to CELEBRATE! Congratulate yourself – you are one step closer to your Z! Each accomplishment is worth marking with a mini-celebration, whatever that is for you. Share it with a friend, post it on social media, do a victory lap around your house, ring a bell, buy your favorite coffee treat, take a nap in the sunshine – whatever feels like a clap-on-the-back – as it will encourage you to do it again. As you reach each goal or milestone, the next ones start to look easier, and you might become bolder and set scarier goals. Check in with the fear – it means you're on to something. Fear and excitement manifest in the body the same way physiologically – butterflies in your stomach, sweaty palms, flushed skin – these are adrenaline reactions to feeling fear *OR* excitement. The difference between the two is your mindset. So, any time you feel scared, remind yourself that you are getting closer to your Z, and turn that fear into excitement instead.

EXERCISE 25:
Your Roadmap to Z

Now that you have identified one action to take that will get you closer to your Z, you might want to expand that into a more detailed action plan. We provide an example below to help you get started. For each of your Bold Goals, start breaking them down into smaller steps that will get you closer to accomplishing it. Identify what area of *Finding Your Z* this goal is aligned to and then outline specific actions you plan to take and create an accountability structure for yourself. Finally, and most importantly, identify how you will celebrate when you complete that action!

YOUR ROADMAP FOR FINDING YOUR Z

BOLD GOAL	ELEMENT OF Z	ACTION	ACCOUNTABILITY	REWARD/ CELEBRATION
Example: Spend a Month in Tuscany, Italy	WHERE	Learn to Speak Italian	Ask my travel partner to take an online Italian class with me	Meal at my favorite Italian restaurant
Example: Spend a Month in Tuscany, Italy	WHERE	Start saving $200 a week for the trip	Deposit it automatically into an account that my best friend manages	Once I save $10,000 I will book my plane ticket and ask for the time off

By the way – another resource for your journey to Z is <u>Us</u>, the authors of this book, as well as the community we are creating full of fellow travelers who are on their own path to Z. Let this community inspire you – share your dreams and challenges with us and let us celebrate your successes! It keeps all of us going! You can join our community through social media or by visiting our website **www.findingyourz. com**. We hope to meet you someday through our coaching programs or at a workshop where we can guide you to go deeper into who you are, what you want, and what is getting in your way.

Finally, don't forget to enjoy the ride. It's like we told Jonathan, being happy is the goal at every letter in your alphabet. Undoubtedly you will encounter detours, roadblocks, and U-turns, just like Kent experienced. But in those moments you can refer back to this book and remind yourself what really matters to you in life, or as Abbi would say, what provides your "sparkle." Make the adjustments and trade-offs that are right for you and your family – the way Mario has always done – and don't be flattered into saying yes to a life you don't want. Check in with your GPS and recalculate your route on a regular basis, as Greg does, and continue to find joy in the journey.

There is value and growth available at every mile marker. When you are in the valley of despair, that's where the deepest learnings happen, just ask Andy and Michael. If you can't find a clearly laid out plan, forge your own, the way Amy did! Don't be in such a rush to get to Z that you forget to look out the window, put the top down, feel the wind in your hair, and let the sun shine on your face. If you have the chance, help others realize their Z too, like the Bishop Brothers are!

We knew in our souls that this book would indeed be written one day. It was a promise we made to ourselves and to each other and every day it wasn't finished it felt like an unchecked box on our life's to-do list. It took us nearly three years, **three years**, to find the time and energy (FUEL) we needed to finish it. But here we are, sitting in sunny Florida on our final writer's retreat, the patio windows covered with Post-it notes and chapter outlines, writing our final sentences. We are dreaming about our book launch party and crying as we write the dedication page. We actually did it, and it feels great! It didn't happen within the timeline we planned, and it took way more energy and grit than predicted, but that's life. The dream never left our hearts, and once we could replenish our fuel, we started down the path again.

You can do hard things too — such as writing a book with your best friend in the middle of a global pandemic.

EXERCISE 26:

Go!

Congratulations — *You are officially on your way to Finding Your Z!* Use this space as your travel journal to capture your learnings along the way.

66 You can't be that kid at the top of the waterslide, overthinking it. You have to go down the chute. **99**

TINA FEY

ACKNOWLEDGMENTS

While we dedicated this book to our daughters, there are two unassuming heroes who helped make this happen – our husbands **Fred & Brent**. They have consistently and actively supported our investment of effort, time, and money to complete this book. They both lovingly took on the role of single parenting while we went on writer's retreats or hid in our homes to write. We love you and could not have completed this labor of love without your support and belief in us. Thank you for helping us find our Z and being our lifelong Bandmates.

The Peeps. The Peeps is how we lovingly refer to our Ride or Die friends – the ones that have known us since we were crazy college kids and have grown up to be our extended family. We thank them for their encouragement, never doubting for one single moment that we would write this book and make it a smashing success! (Who are we kidding, there were moments). There is no one else we would rather have in our "Band" than The Peeps – Sarah, Jameson, Staci, Steve, Dan, Abby, Dave, Dennis, Janelle and our angel in heaven, Colin.

Our extended families, siblings, in-laws and parents - for believing in us and encouraging us to keep going! We would not be where and who we are without you. We love you!

Tyler and Timmy Bishop. As you read in the book, we met them when this book was just a dream and some scribbles on Post-It notes and flipcharts. Tyler immediately understood the importance of the message and helped us bring it to life in the beautiful photos and moving videos that we share on our website. Tyler introduced us to his brother Timmy who became our earliest fan and social media guru. His work and dedication helped us launch our first ever *Finding Your Z* workshop and we are forever grateful for his early support and the hustle that set our dreams in flight. The Bishop Brothers are Dreamers and they are going places. Check out their website at http://www.tylerbishopstudios.com.

OUR MOVIE STARS!

Amy Schweim. Amy was our very first star, and guinea pig, in the *Finding Your Z* video series. Her support and patience with us was amazing as we figured out how to shoot hours of video footage and turn it into a meaningful story. The hours and hours she spent with us all over Durango, Colorado became the inspiration for other stories to follow and we are so grateful for the time and energy she put in to helping us launch our website and book. Check out her website to learn about the cool business she has built at: www.womensradicalpursuits.com

Andy and Michael Nelson. Andy and Michael have been so generous in their support of *Finding Your Z* and in sharing their very personal, beautiful story about Andy's battle with cancer. You will never meet more whole-hearted people than the Nelsons and we are so grateful for their friendship and support. They are also writing a book about their journey, called the Gifts of Cancer. You can check it out at: www.thegiftsofcancer.com.

Abbi Panasuk. Abbi generously opened up her home and welcomed us in to interview her, her family, and her team for one of our *Finding Your Z* video stories. Abbi embodies every aspect of *Finding Your Z* and we are so honored to have been able to tell her story. We are sure that you will be inspired by the intentional life she has built.

Thank you to **Matt Jewett** for taking our PowerPoint ideas and turning them into the graphics we needed to make this book come to life. Your eye for design is a gift we are so grateful for!

Thank you to the team at **Book Baby**, specifically Kim Sherry, for helping us get this book published without pulling our hair out.

And finally, to Candyce's team at **The People Side**, Michelle's colleagues at **Post Consumer Brands,** and our personal Life Coaches – **Anni Boyum, Michelle Stimpson and Liv Lane** – thank you for pouring your wisdom and encouragement into us. We would not be where we are without you.

ABOUT THE AUTHORS

CANDYCE PENTEADO

Candyce has spent the majority of her career standing in front of full classrooms and audiences all over the world. Whether you are coaching with her one-on-one, or learning from her in an audience with hundreds of other people, she will keep you engaged and entertained. Her humorous and wholehearted approach helps people feel personally connected to her message and compelled to go live their life on purpose. She is the founder and Managing Partner of The People Side, a leadership development and executive coaching practice, and co-author of the book *Finding Your Z*. Candyce lives in Minnesota with her husband and two daughters.

MICHELLE NEWMAN

Michelle is a certified coach with a 20+ year track record of helping people develop professionally and leading life changing conversations. She has deep expertise in helping people navigate career decisions and accomplish their personal and professional goals. She is on her personal path to Z by helping other people change their lives one letter at a time. Michelle is an HR leader at Post Consumer Brands and co-author of the book *Finding Your Z*. She lives in Minnesota with her husband and three daughters.